TWO CENTURIES

GENERAL EDITOR: MICHAEL SCAIFE, M.A.

THE SECOND WORLD WAR

M. J. A. MORTIMORE, B.A.

Senior History Master
Bridlington School

University Tutorial Press

Published 1974

© M. J. A. Mortimore, 1974

Set in 10 on 12pt Plantin

Printed in Great Britain by University Tutorial Press Ltd,
Foxton, near Cambridge

ISBN: 0 7231 0589 8

940·53

UNIVERSITY TUTORIAL PRESS LTD
9-10 Great Sutton Street
London, EC1V 0DA

CONTENTS

ACKNOWLEDGMENTS

The author is grateful to the following for permission to reproduce photographs, each of which is individually acknowledged in the text:

Imperial War Museum (also Cover Picture).

Radio Times Hulton Picture Library.

ALL QUIET ON THE WESTERN FRONT?

When the First World War ended, the world was not blind to the possibility that there might one day be another. In 1919 the League of Nations was established to keep the peace, and agreement to support this organisation was written into the actual treaties which ended the war. Nor was this all. France and some of Germany's eastern neighbours, notably Poland and Czechoslovakia, exchanged promises of mutual support; in 1925, by the Locarno treaties, Germany agreed with other Powers to guarantee the existing Franco-Belgian-German frontiers; and in 1926 Germany herself was admitted as a member to the League of Nations. Yet all these "guarantees" were to prove inadequate.

The peace treaties and the League of Nations had a great many built-in weaknesses. The United States Senate having refused to ratify the Treaty of Versailles, the U.S.A. took no part in the League, and withdrew into a position of lofty isolation. Russia, under its new Communist government, was widely regarded with suspicion. The war was hardly over before Britain and France were quarrelling bitterly over the Middle East and the amount of war reparations Germany should be forced to pay. Finally, the newly-independent states of central Europe, which had come into existence with the collapse of Tsarist Russia and the break-up of the old Austro-Hungarian empire, were a standing temptation to their greedier and more powerful neighbours, Soviet Russia and—eventually—Nazi Germany.

To make matters worse, the twenties and thirties were on the whole a period of world-wide trade depression, when unemployment and poverty were widespread. Beset by economic problems which threatened their very existence, governments became increasingly wrapped up in their own selfish concerns, and increasingly indifferent to the problems of Europe as a whole. This was the fundamental tragedy.

Rearmament or Disarmament?

Moreover, the Treaty of Versailles itself created difficulties. As one of the victorious Allies, Italy had been promised various benefits, which the Treaty in fact failed to grant her. An impoverished country at the best of times, it is not hard to understand Italy's disillusionment and bitterness in the post-war years. The result was that she quickly succumbed to the showy promises of the dictator Mussolini and his Fascist Party. On the other side, the Treaty had imposed severe restrictions on the future armed forces of Germany. She was to be permitted no submarines or military aircraft, only a tiny surface fleet, and a small army which was not to be allowed within 50 kilometres of the Rhine. These terms were both unrealistic and vindictive, and left the Germans with a strong sense of grievance. Stripped for the time being of their status as a great Power, they felt anger and humiliation. Meanwhile, economic difficulties caused hardship which extremist politicians of every kind exploited, and people were increasingly attracted to parties— however unscrupulous—which promised radical solutions to Germany's problems. This helps to explain the rise of Hitler and the Nazis to power in 1933.

For a long time Hitler was something of an enigma. Although his views were highly alarming, few were disposed to take them seriously or to believe that once in office prudence would not compel him to modify them. Hitler had declared in *Mein Kampf* his abhorrence of Jews and Communists, his belief in a master race (*Herrenvolk*) designed by nature to dominate all others, and his conviction that Germany must have a "final reckoning" with France. He also proclaimed that the Germans had a right to more living space (*Lebensraum*), and soon declared his intention of rearming Germany with or without the League's consent.

Although the Führer's words reflected German grievances over the Treaty of Versailles, Europe remained, if not unconcerned, at any rate undecided. Many felt that the Germans, and more especially the Italians, had indeed had a raw deal in 1919; and so they preferred to see only the better side of the Nazi and Fascist governments. Others, while noting and deploring their militaristic tendencies, nevertheless declared that it would be immoral for the rest of Europe to imitate them. There was in fact a strong European movement in the 1930s in favour of disarmament, especially on the political left wing. People wanted peace. It was believed that the arms race between the rival European powers had been an important cause of the First World War; and there were therefore considerable pressures operating to deter democratic governments from the use of force. Clearly, then, at this point the dictators had little to fear.

Two significant events soon focused attention on the dangers of this situation. The first was Mussolini's invasion of Abyssinia (1935). This blatant act of aggression, a product of Il Duce's ambition to make Italy an imperial Power, provoked only an ineffectual response from the League. Sanctions were imposed;

but oil, the one necessity Italy was without, was not among them. The conquest therefore proceeded as planned. Then in 1936 came Hitler's remilitarisation of the Rhineland, his first open defiance of the Treaty of Versailles. German guns once more overlooked French soil. Hitler was warned by his anxious generals that France could still defeat Germany single-handed; he replied that the French would do nothing, and events proved him right. After that, the contrast between Hitler's readiness to gamble and others' indecision was clear: he became convinced that other nations would not agree to act together, and were afraid to act alone.

But ordinary citizens, especially in the U.S.A. and Britain, greeted the lack of effective action over Abyssinia and the Rhineland with protest and disgust. Many had already begun to see the world situation as a conflict of principle between totalitarian, Fascist-style regimes and more democratic ones, between "the dictators" and "the people"—a conflict crystallised in the Spanish Civil War which broke out in 1936. Leaders of the Spanish army, with aims similar to those of the Fascists, rose in revolt against the legitimate republican government of Spain, and were at once supported by Rome and Berlin. Individual sympathisers with the Republican cause rushed to join the International Brigades, and "fight for democracy"; but for the governments themselves the moment for action had already passed. Shaken and divided by the ruthless opportunism of the dictators, conscious of the political unpopularity of rearmament, the democracies were profoundly alarmed by the great devastation caused to undefended Spanish cities by German and Italian bombers. They therefore preferred not to risk war with the dictators, hoping that they would by this policy of appeasement reduce the international tensions created by Germany and Italy.

Ironically, this feeling that appeasement might be wiser than resistance owed a good deal to its chief opponents. Those who had long advocated rearmament by the democracies, like Winston Churchill in Britain, had also consistently exaggerated the strength of Nazi forces—and thereby played Hitler's game of bluff for him. They certainly contributed to many people's anxiety to avoid a confrontation with the dictators, as crisis now rapidly succeeded crisis. Many European countries already contained pro-Nazi parties, and these were soon to be used as the basis for Hitler's claims on other people's territory. The first victim was Austria, already the scene of an unsuccessful Nazi coup in 1934, following the assassination of Chancellor Dollfuss. Now, in March 1938, acting under orders from Hitler and backed up by German troops, Austrian Nazis seized power and proclaimed *Anschluss* (political union between Austria and Germany).

Next on the list was Czechoslovakia. Here the excuse for action was the alleged persecution by the Czechs of the German-speaking population of Sudetenland, a part of Czechoslovakia bordering on Germany. By now, Hitler's generals were so alarmed at what they saw as a grave risk of war, that they actually plotted to overthrow him through a military revolt; but at that very moment the British and French governments fearfully pressed the Czechs to give up Sudetenland, and the generals' plot naturally collapsed. The Czech surrender was then agreed to at the Munich conference in September 1938, and Prime Minister Chamberlain returned home saying, "I believe it is peace in our time". Hitler, intoxicated by the ease of his successes, shared this belief. He did not want a war and it appeared that no one was prepared to fight him. He was totally unprepared psychologically for the sudden change which was about to come.

For in fact the Munich agreement marked the end of the policy of appeasement. Not content with Munich, within three weeks Hitler had begun planning the

4th May, 1939: Duxford, Cambridgeshire. Preparing for war, pilots practise scrambling to their Spitfires. (Radio Times Hulton Picture Library)

seizure of the rest of Czechoslovakia, and the Baltic ports of Memel and Danzig. Faced with this situation, the attitude of the French and British hardened at last: Munich must be their final concession. In March 1939 German troops occupied Prague. It was obvious that Poland would be Hitler's next target, and in the same month Britain and France, which had been rearming, declared that any threat to Poland would be met by immediate resistance. This abrupt, even bewildering, reversal of attitude made a war virtually inevitable. Hitler would be certain to call what past experience told him was a bluff, and the western Powers could not help Poland except by attacking Germany. Next month the Italians invaded Albania, and the Allies replied with promises of support to Greece. The big question now was, what would the Russians do? They had, after all, a non-aggression treaty with Poland. On August 24th the world knew the answer: a Nazi-Soviet Pact had been signed, cynically giving the two parties a free hand to seize Polish territory. The democracies now knew exactly where they stood, and war was just a week away.

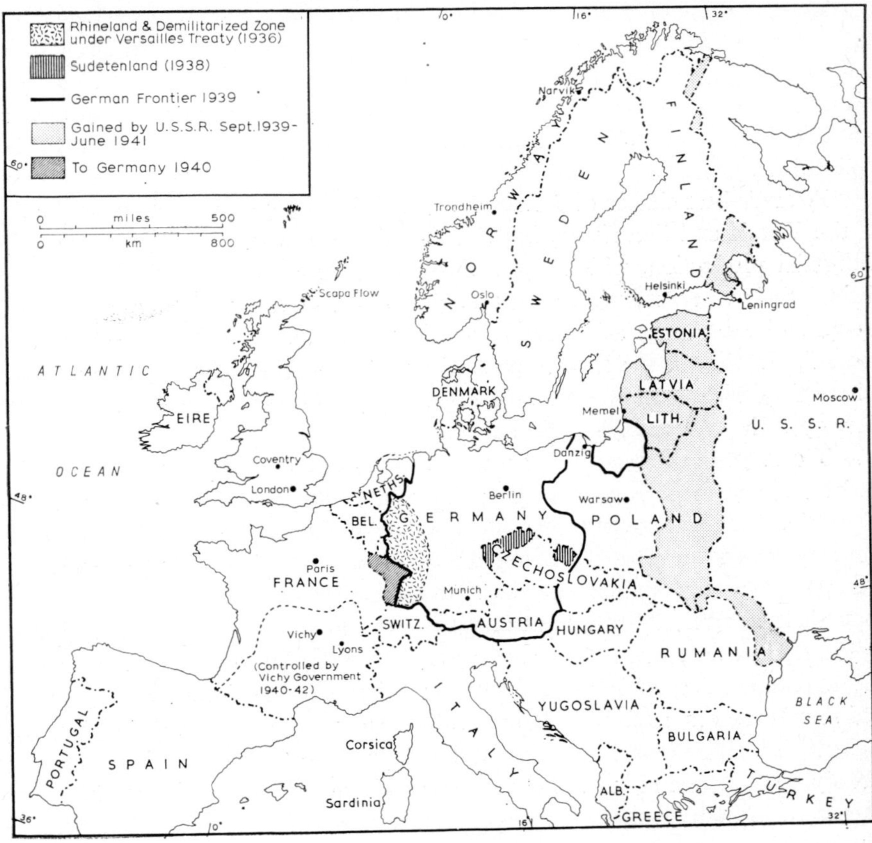

Changes in Europe

"BLITZKRIEG"

The Fate of Poland

Hitler's invasion of Poland began on September 1st 1939. It led two days later to a declaration of war by Britain and France, and the departure for Europe of a British Expeditionary Force, but Hitler's plan was to crush Poland so quickly that Britain and France would think again about fighting Germany. His Army Group North (630,000 men and 800 aircraft under Col.-Gen. von Bock) was to attack across the Polish Corridor, and swing south towards Warsaw and Brest-Litovsk; Army Group South (886,000 men and 600 aircraft commanded by von Rundstedt) was to drive eastwards before turning to join von Bock behind Polish lines.

Poland's best chance of defence lay in fighting a holding action along the line of the Vistula and San rivers, but this would mean sacrificing the main areas of industrial production, which lay further west. The Poles therefore decided to defend their whole frontier, even though this meant the wide dispersal of their troops and consequent lack of any counter-attack force. Nothing could have been more fatal: though the Poles mobilised over one million men, they had cavalry where they needed tanks, and were opposed by an enemy whose strategists had developed the *"blitzkrieg"*—lightning war.

The *"blitzkrieg"* had three aspects. First came the bombers, used as a kind of aerial artillery to destroy strategic points and terrorise the civilian population. Then the tanks and storm troops broke through, aiming to penetrate deeply into the country and envelop the defenders from the rear. These armoured thrusts were supported by dive-bombers, whose screaming sirens were more unnerving than their bombs. Finally the ground-troops mopped up pockets of resistance by-passed by the armour. True to pattern, in the first forty-eight hours of the war the Luftwaffe (German Air Force) destroyed many Polish aircraft on the ground, and then turned to demolish communications, so that the Poles could neither complete their mobilisation nor satisfactorily deploy the troops they had mobilised already. By September 17th the spectacular advance of General Heinz Guderian's Panzer corps had virtually completed the encirclement of the defenders with the capture of Brest-Litovsk, and on the same day two Russian Army Groups invaded

Poland from the east as foreshadowed by the Nazi-Soviet Pact. Only about 100,000 Polish troops evaded this double onslaught. Before the end of the month Poland had disappeared from the map, partitioned between the two conquerors, who with characteristic effrontery then declared this arrangement an ideal basis for a lasting peace in Europe.

The Winter War

Despite this, Stalin was uneasy about Hitler's future intentions. Leningrad was potentially vulnerable to a sudden German attack but might be protected by a

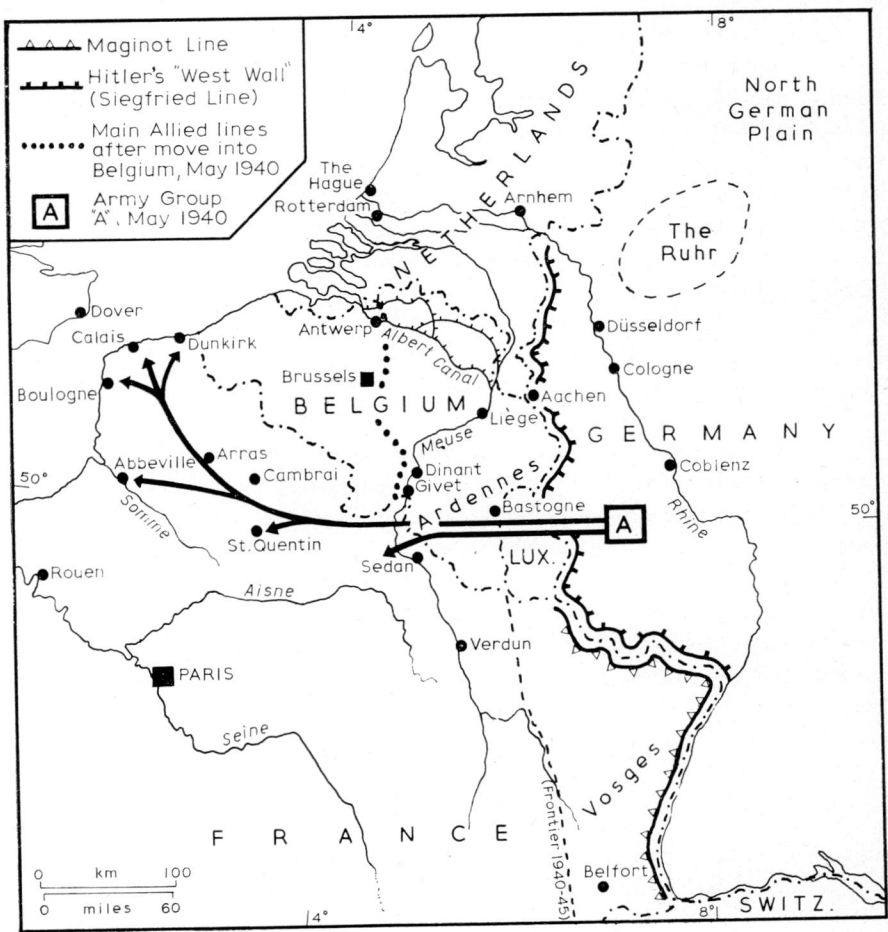

The Western Front 1939-40

further extension of Soviet territory. Estonia, Latvia and Lithuania, states which Hitler had agreed should become a Russian sphere of influence, quickly submitted and accepted Russian garrisons; Finland, however, rejected Soviet approaches based on an exchange of territory. Stalin then resorted to Hitler's methods. The Russians accused the Finns of attacking them, and used this fiction as an excuse for heavy air raids on Helsinki and large-scale attacks by land. This was on November 30th.

The Finns raised a total of 200,000 men, only a fifth of the opposing Russian force. But the Finnish troops employed tactics of tight encirclement ideally suited to the wooded landscape and severe weather. In this way, small Finnish ski-borne forces more than once defeated and even destroyed whole Soviet divisions. In the meantime, the British and French governments seriously considered mounting an expedition to aid Finland—a move which would certainly have led to war against the U.S.S.R. and did strain Allied relations with Norway and Sweden, through whose territory the Anglo-French forces would have passed. Fortunately for them, the campaign was over before they had taken any action. In the New Year the Russians threw in a fresh army, concentrated on the Karelian isthmus north of Leningrad, and the Finns at last asked for an armistice. By the Treaty of Moscow (March 1940) Finland was obliged to hand over most of the territory where fighting had taken place.

"Phoney War" in the West

Meanwhile, there had been little activity in western Europe, so little that American newspaper correspondents soon began describing this as "the phoney war". Bad weather and the opposition of his generals continually frustrated Hitler's plans for an attack in the West, until an apparently unlucky accident compelled him to change them altogether. For their part, the Allies were remarkably complacent, though with little enough reason. Despite being faced by relatively weak German forces, the Allies remained predominantly on the defensive, putting their trust in prepared fortifications such as the "impregnable" Maginot Line.

Consequently the excitement, such as it was during the winter of 1939-40, was provided by the war at sea. A notable German exploit, for example, was that of Lieutenant Prien and the submarine U-47, in entering the British anchorage at Scapa Flow and sinking the battleship *Royal Oak*. Then it was Britain's turn. In December, the German pocket battleship *Admiral Graf Spee* was brought to bay by three cruisers off the River Plate; fearing its loss, Hitler ordered it to be scuttled. Two months later the *Altmark*, former supply ship to the *Graf Spee*,

February 1940. Officers and men of H.M. Ships Ajax and Exeter inspected by the King and Queen and congratulated on their defeat of the Graf Spee. (Radio Times Hulton Picture Library)

with 300 British prisoners aboard, was taken in Norwegian territorial waters in an episode soon to have far-reaching consequences.

The cry of "The Navy's here!", which had greeted the British seamen locked in the holds of the *Altmark*, cheered many at home who had ached for something to applaud. So far the war had been a pretty depressing experience. Families had been broken up by the evacuation of city children to safe areas in the country; the "blackout" made travel after dark difficult and dangerous; the A.R.P. ("Air Raid Precautions") Warden was often regarded as just another official nosey-parker; food rationing had begun; posters warned that "Careless Talk Costs Lives"; and everyone was obliged to go about his business with his gas mask in an ungainly cardboard box.

1st September 1939. Schoolchildren are evacuated from London.
(Radio Times Hulton Picture Library)

The Norwegian Campaign

The *Altmark* affair, coming so soon after the Anglo-French plan for an expedition to Finland, strained relations between Britain and Norway. But it also convinced Hitler that Britain intended to disregard Norwegian neutrality and even contemplated an actual invasion. This indeed was true, for plans were being drawn up to mine Norway's territorial waters, through which Swedish iron ore was carried to Germany from the Norwegian port of Narvik. Hitler could not afford to risk any Allied intervention—so he decided to strike first.

Accordingly, audacious plans were made for landings at eight separate points on April 9th 1940. Denmark, in the path of the invasion, surrendered without a fight. The Norwegians, however, were made of sterner stuff: the ancient guns at Oslo sank the heavy cruiser *Blücher* and delayed the landings long enough for the government to escape from the city and organise resistance. During the next few days the British fleet belatedly sank a dozen German warships, including the whole of the force which had landed troops at Narvik. The effective German fleet at that point in time was reduced to three cruisers and four destroyers. On land, however, it was a different story. Despite the landing of some 12,000 British and French troops north and south of Trondheim, they were easily driven out by smaller German forces with superior air support. Only at Narvik, inaccessible by land and almost beyond range for the all-conquering Luftwaffe, were the Allies successful in repulsing the Germans; but by then (the end of May) the news from France was so bad that it was decided to abandon Norway to the enemy.

"Blitzkrieg" in the West

Meanwhile the Allied armies in France had missed their opportunity. The original 33 German divisions facing them had now increased to 136, but the Allies were still not outnumbered. Contrary to popular belief, for example, the French alone possessed more and heavier tanks than the Germans, but they had not realised the need to concentrate them. They had also failed to appreciate the extent to which a modern army depends for its effectiveness on air cover, and had neglected anti-aircraft defences, whereas the Germans had developed a much feared dive-bomber in the famous *Stuka*. Yet it remains true that the Germans were not overwhelmingly superior; what followed was much more a question of mobility and outlook than of equipment.

The Allies believed the main German attack would come through northern Belgium, which was confirmed when a German plane carrying orders to this effect was forced down in Belgium, which was then neutral. The French and British therefore planned to move forward into Belgium at the first sign of a German assault. Convinced that the Ardennes forest was in itself a major obstacle to an enemy, they proposed to defend the area between Givet and the Maginot Line with comparatively weak forces. Meanwhile, however, influenced by Generals von Manstein and Guderian, Hitler had adopted a new and better plan to replace that captured by the Allies. This new plan involved a principal thrust with powerful concentrations of armour through the weakly-defended Ardennes towards Sedan and on to the Channel, which if successful would split the Allied forces clean in two. For this purpose, von Rundstedt's Army Group A was increased to 44 divisions, 7 of them armoured.

The attack therefore began on May 10th with the Allies theoretically strong on the flanks but undeniably weak in the centre, and moreover with inadequately mobile reserves. On the German right, the Netherlands succumbed after a short struggle, their substantial army out-manoeuvred by airborne German forces, and their population unnerved by savage air raids on Rotterdam and the Hague. Parachutists and glider troops were also effective in Belgium, where they landed on top of the much-vaunted Fort Eben-Emael and forced its surrender with ridiculous

May 1940. *Refugees fleeing before the German invasion in Northern France.*
(*Radio Times Hulton Picture Library*)

ease. Then, crossing the River Meuse and the Albert Canal north of Liège, von Bock's Army Group B, though only a subsidiary force of 28 divisions, attacked with such fury that the Allies continued to regard this as the main assault. The real shock, however, was still to come, as Army Group A approached the weak spot in the Allied centre. On May 13th Guderian's XIX Panzer Corps crossed the Meuse at Sedan, and in seven unbelievable days had reached the Channel. Guderian's exploitation of his success—even against resistance from his own High Command—was the crux of the whole battle, which was finally decided when the French failed to move quickly enough to the counter-attack.

The situation for the Allies was now serious: 40 of their best divisions were trapped in Belgium. A breakthrough to the south was a forlorn hope, but as the collapse of the Belgians on the Allied left began to appear imminent, even that slender chance receded. All that remained was evacuation through the one

Channel port left open, Dunkirk, a desperate though heroic enterprise which even then was only made possible because at the crucial moment Hitler, suddenly and surprisingly, decided to halt the German armour. Over 300,000 Allied troops escaped, including almost the entire British Expeditionary Force which, however, had to leave all its equipment behind. Almost at once, two British divisions were sent back to France, where French armies under General Weygand were struggling to make a new line along the Somme and the Aisne; but again the German armour soon broke through, and as before the defenders were forced to retreat to protect their flanks. The remaining British troops in France were evacuated. By June 17th Guderian had reached the Swiss frontier, cutting off half a million French

June 1940. *Evacuation from Dunkirk. British and French troops waiting for destroyers to take them back to England.*
(Radio Times Hulton Picture Library)

soldiers still held uselessly in the Maginot Line—and meanwhile, judging his moment to a nicety, Mussolini had declared war on the Allies.

Thus the theories of von Manstein and Guderian were more than justified. Poland had convinced them that given a sufficient concentration of rapidly-moving and long-ranging tanks, penetration could be achieved so deep that the armoured units would emerge into open country well behind the enemy's rearmost positions. Once that was accomplished, the potential threat to the German flanks could safely be ignored: as the French campaign showed, the defenders would be far too concerned about their own communications to appreciate the weakness of the Germans'. So France was made to pay a bitter price for the political weakness of pre-war years. On June 17th a new French government established at Vichy under the veteran Marshal Pétain asked Germany for an armistice, hoping through collaboration with the invaders to preserve at least a semblance of independence, and to avert the worst features of a military occupation.

"Somewhere in England 1940." Spitfires taking off to intercept German aircraft.
(Radio Times Hulton Picture Library)

"THEIR FINEST HOUR"

Britain under Siege

The collapse of their continental allies left the British to fight Hitler alone. However, they did so under the leadership of a new government: widespread dissatisfaction over the handling of the Norwegian campaign resulted in the replacement of Chamberlain's Conservative ministry by a coalition led by his First Lord of the Admiralty, Winston Churchill, with the leader of the Labour Party, Clement Attlee, as Deputy Prime Minister. Two Conservatives and one Labour M.P. completed the War Cabinet of five. Fifteen other offices of cabinet rank went to Conservatives, four to Labour and one to the Liberals. Two notable appointments were those of Lord Beaverbrook, owner of the *Daily Express*, as Minister of Aircraft Production, and Ernest Bevin, general secretary of the Transport and General Workers' Union, as Minister of Labour. This pooling of the nation's talents gave the people confidence in their government for the rest of the war.

The new Prime Minister, whose oratory was to stir the public to undreamed-of efforts, painted a sufficiently gloomy picture of Britain's prospects in that summer of 1940—"I have nothing to offer but blood, toil, tears and sweat"—but the fact was that Hitler had his problems, too. Until July he continued to hope that Britain would make peace, and may even have permitted the escape from Dunkirk partly for that reason. When British determination to fight on was made clear, therefore, Hitler had no alternative but to attempt an invasion of Britain for which he was totally unprepared.

The plan depended on the Luftwaffe being able to establish a superiority in the air sufficient to counterbalance the weakness of the German Navy compared with the British. Goering, the Luftwaffe Commander-in-Chief, believed this was possible, and Churchill was under no illusions as to the significance of the contest to come: "The Battle of France is over. I expect that the Battle of Britain is about to begin." The Germans' plan throughout was to destroy the R.A.F. fighters, so as to give their own bombers a clear field to prepare the way for invasion. They hoped to do this in daylight, first by enticing the R.A.F. to engage in large-scale battles over the south coast, and then by bombing the fighter stations themselves.

When the battle began in mid-July, the Luftwaffe had a substantial advantage in overall numbers, but not in terms of fighters alone; and since daylight raids required fighter escort, that meant the Germans were only able to deploy about half their bomber strength for this operation. Moreover, the Luftwaffe had won its reputation mainly in a ground-support role, and the Battle of Britain was to be its first experience of action against an organised air defence. Besides, the German Messerschmitt 109 had an operational radius which barely allowed it to reach London, while the R.A.F., operating often over its own bases, could stay in action longer. Finally, the new British system of radio-location (radar) enabled Air Chief Marshal Dowding's Fighter Command to guide the fighters to the attack on the basis of a complete picture of German movements, whereas the enemy had no system of ground-control at all.

As a result, the Germans suffered total losses almost twice as heavy as those of the R.A.F. Furthermore, under the direction of Lord Beaverbrook, newspaper tycoon turned Minister of Aircraft Production, British factories outpaced their German counterparts. Pilots, not planes, were crucial, with weekly losses running up to over 10%. But by early September—when a final, mistaken attempt to reach a decision by switching the attack to London relieved the desperate pressure on Fighter Command and its exhausted pilots—the Luftwaffe had shot its bolt. It was Hitler's first defeat. In October the invasion was cancelled: "Never in the field of human conflict," said Churchill, "was so much owed by so many to so few." However, Germany's naval weakness makes it doubtful whether an invasion would have succeeded even if the Luftwaffe had won the Battle of Britain.

Nevertheless, the Battle of Britain was not the whole story. German "blitzes" by night, while of little strategic effectiveness, caused considerable damage and loss of life among civilians, and anxiety to servicemen parted from their families. They also gave the whole population, men and women, the feeling that they were in the "front line" with a vital job to do—as firewatchers, rescue workers, members of the Home Guard, Air Raid Wardens, Special Constables, volunteer firemen, ambulance drivers, or rest-centre helpers. At Coventry, for example, 554 died in a raid on November 14th which destroyed whole areas of the city; and over the next six months most large towns suffered heavy bombing.

The Battle of Britain aroused great admiration in the U.S.A., where the dictators were far from popular. Early in the war, Walter Winchell, the widely-read newspaper columnist, had spoken for many Americans when he said, "I'm absolutely neutral, I don't care who kills Hitler." For his part, Churchill believed in cultivating the Americans. "Give us the tools," he declared in a broadcast in February 1941, "and we will finish the job." The American President, Roosevelt, had agreed to the idea of "lend-lease", by which the U.S.A. would supply goods without demanding payment in cash. On the other hand, there was a strong isolationist group in the U.S.A. determined to avoid American involvement in a war which they regarded as none of their business, and it was therefore a notable victory for Churchill and Roosevelt when the Lend-Lease Act became law in

March 1941. This Act led to a closer liaison between the two English-speaking powers, and thus paved the way for actual American participation in the war, and eventual victory. More immediately, the agreement had already provided Britain with fifty old but valuable destroyers for use against German submarines in the Atlantic, where U-boats were now hunting by night in "wolf-packs" on the surface and causing heavy losses to British merchant shipping.

Unable to produce for themselves more than a fraction of their needs in food and materials, the British had long understood the importance of protecting their seaborne trade, both against U-boats and conventional warships. An epic chase in May 1941 ended with the destruction of the formidable new German battleship *Bismarck*, though at the tragic cost of the battle cruiser *Hood* and all but three of her crew. Other surface raiders—*Lutzow, Prinz Eugen, Scharnhorst*, and *Gneisenau* —were crippled from the air, and the threat was over for the present.

The Mediterranean

Meanwhile, the entry of Italy into the war at once made the Mediterranean a vital strategic area, and laid a heavy burden on the Royal Navy. Mussolini, like the ancient Romans he strove to imitate, thirsted for conquest, but his bungling attacks in Greece and Africa merely succeeded in drawing Hitler into fresh campaigns he would have preferred to avoid. The Italian invasion of Greece in October 1940 was soon halted by the Greeks, and with the aid of British air forces pushed back well into Albania. Nevertheless, Hitler could not allow his ally to be humiliated indefinitely, nor could he risk the presence of British bombers within striking distance of his chief oilfields at Ploesti in Rumania; so he decided to intervene (April 1941). The governments of Hungary, Rumania and Bulgaria had already aligned themselves with Germany, and Yugoslavia was invaded simultaneously, so that German forces were able to outflank the Greek and British positions from the north-east. The Greeks were cut off and forced to surrender after a fortnight, while the 50,000 British survivors were evacuated to Crete by the Royal Navy.

From the Navy's point of view, the fall of France had meant the loss of important bases in the western Mediterranean, and the potential opposition of the powerful French fleet there. The Italian fleet alone was stronger than Admiral Cunningham's whole force in the Mediterranean, and the vital British base at Malta was therefore extremely vulnerable from the sea and the air. Hence the government decided that supplies for the Middle East must go by the long route round the Cape of Good Hope, and, reluctantly, that the French ships must be destroyed to prevent them falling into the wrong hands (July 1940). In November, aircraft from the carrier *Illustrious* successfully attacked the Italian fleet at Taranto, and in March 1941 Cunningham accounted for five more vessels off Cape Matapan in a brilliant night action. However, with the arrival of the Germans on the scene air superiority passed decisively to them. Not only was Malta heavily bombed month after month from bases less than 20 minutes away, but Cunningham's fleet was hamstrung by having to work largely at night. This German air superiority was soon convincingly demonstrated in Crete, attacked in May 1941 and captured by airborne forces alone, in the first great confrontation between air- and sea-power in history. The decision rested on a knife-edge, for initially a mere 3,000 of General Student's paratroops were matched against 28,000 British defenders; but the decisive factor was German ability to bring in reinforcements by air whereas Cunningham dared not do so by sea—a lesson emphasised by the loss of nine ships while evacuating the survivors. But the Navy destroyed a German sea-borne support force, and succeeded in evacuating over half the British troops. German casualties as a whole were so much heavier than they anticipated that Hitler began to doubt whether airborne operations on this scale were really worthwhile.

Top: Italy 1943-45
Below: The Mediterranean 1939-45

1940.   Life in a destroyer: listening to the news on the wireless.
(Radio Times Hulton Picture Library)

The loss of Crete left Africa, long the scene of colonial rivalry between the powers, as the only area where land operations were in progress, chiefly in the narrow strip bordering the Mediterranean where the coast road provided essential communications.   In September 1940 seven Italian divisions under Marshal Graziani had advanced from Libya into British-dominated Egypt, but were soon halted around Sidi Barrani by inadequate communications.   In December the British, commanded by General Sir Archibald Wavell, decided on a counter-attack. Wavell could only call on the two divisions of the Western Desert Force under General O'Connor, but surprise was complete and O'Connor had 275 tanks to the Italians' 120, so that Bardia and Tobruk with its valuable harbour were soon taken. A spectacular dash across country by the 7th Armoured Division then cut off the Italian retreat at Beda Fomm, and in February 1941 they surrendered.   O'Connor had taken 135,000 prisoners, with hundreds of tanks, guns and vehicles, for the loss of only 2,000 men killed, wounded and missing.

After this, Wavell turned his attention to Italian East Africa, where by May a quarter of a million enemy troops (including natives) in Abyssinia, Eritrea and

Somaliland had been obliged to surrender. The Italian failure in the desert, however, had meanwhile persuaded Hitler to attempt a "rescue operation" with two divisions under the command of General Erwin Rommel. Circumstances thus created grave problems for Wavell. Besides taking the offensive in East Africa, he was instructed by Churchill to send all available troops to Greece, when he could have pushed on to Tripoli and perhaps have prevented the Germans from landing at all. A heavy price was to be paid for this mistake.

His resources thus depleted, Wavell hoped that the Germans would not be ready to attack him until the summer, but he underestimated his ingenious opponent. On March 31st 1941 Rommel launched an offensive which—though relying heavily on bluff—in less than a fortnight recovered almost all the territory lost by the Italians in the winter. Tobruk, however, remained in British hands, cut off except by sea. Much now depended on which side could be reinforced most effectively, and Churchill was determined on Rommel's defeat, whereas at that time Berlin tended to regard the desert war as of only minor importance. Accordingly, Wavell was ready first; but he soon found that his freshly-equipped armoured units had no answer to Rommel's 88 mm. guns, which were superior to anything on the British side, and the offensive had therefore to be called off.

The attack had been mounted hastily, and Wavell had also been distracted by the need to deal with pro-German elements in Iraq and Syria. Moreover, Wavell and Churchill had never really seen eye to eye, and the result was that in June 1941 Britain's most successful general was replaced. Nevertheless, British prospects were brighter than they had been a year previously. Britain herself was secure, and politically Churchill's personal efforts had established closer contacts with the American government which were soon to yield greater dividends than the Lend-Lease Act. Meanwhile, Germany's lack of a real fleet meant she could not replenish her dwindling stocks of vital materials from abroad and, thanks to Hitler, in the summer of 1941 Britain found herself alone no longer.

THE ROAD TO STALINGRAD

Germany versus Russia

In June 1941 Hitler made what was probably the greatest single blunder of his career: he invaded Russia. Since this act led eventually to the war on two fronts which Germany traditionally feared, and which Hitler himself had always striven to avoid, his motives deserve careful examination. The decision was by no means a sudden one. Hitler had always intended eventually to seek *lebensraum* ("living space") for the German people in western Russia and he had never attempted to conceal his belief that Communism was an international menace. The Nazi-Soviet Pact of 1939 represented temporary convenience rather than a change of heart, and the two parties to the Pact remained suspicious of each other. During 1940, Hitler grew anxious over Stalin's seizure of Estonia, Latvia, Lithuania and parts of Rumania. Meanwhile, the sweeping German successes in the West had secured her position in Europe, and made an attack on Russia seem a practical proposition. Moreover, both nations coveted the natural resources of neighbouring countries: Russo-German rivalry ran from the Balkans to the Baltic, from the oilfields of Rumania to the nickel mines of Finland, so it is probably true to say that war between the two powers was more or less inevitable.

Hitler signed the directive for the invasion of Russia—to be known as "Operation Barbarossa"—in December 1940. The plan was to encircle the Russians and destroy their forces as near as possible to their western frontiers, thus denying them any prospect of escape into the vast spaces of Russia as in Napoleon's time, and depriving them of their main European centres of production. The invasion was originally intended to start on May 15th 1941, but the anti-Nazi rising in Yugoslavia in March caused a postponement until June 22nd, a delay that was to have dramatic and in the end fatal consequences for Germany.

The attack found the Russian people psychologically unprepared. Stalin had deliberately concealed the prospect of a conflict with Germany, in the hope that it could be avoided by steering clear of any kind of provocation. He ignored warnings from Britain and the U.S.A. The result was that the invasion came as a crushing shock to the Russians, an important factor in explaining the initial German triumphs. In men and materials they were not significantly inferior to

German leaders studying a map. L. to R. Goering, Keitel, Hitler and Ribbentrop.
(Imperial War Museum)

the Germans: they had, for example, three times as many tanks, one of which, the T 34, was superior to any on the other side. However, there were grave deficiencies in the Soviet army, especially in leadership at all levels, whereas the Germans were particularly skilled exponents of just that kind of mobile warfare most likely to expose the weaknesses of a Soviet army still suffering from Stalin's purges of the 1930s. Moreover, the Nazis conducted their campaign with a degree of ruthlessness which had been absent in western Europe. German troops were officially ordered to treat the Russians as an inferior species and notices at the roadside exhorted them to remember that "Russians must die so that we may live".

The German Attack (June–December 1941)

The invading forces consisted of three groups of armies: Army Group North, commanded by Field-Marshal von Leeb, Army Group Centre under Field-Marshal von Bock, and Army Group South under Field-Marshal von Rundstedt. Their task was to destroy the Russian armies west of a line formed by the Dvina and Dnieper rivers, through a series of encirclements closing near Leningrad,

Smolensk and Kiev, and with this in mind the attack was to be spearheaded by four Panzer groups, larger versions of the armoured formations which had proved so successful in France.

For their part, the Russians were badly organised for defence. Though they possessed in the "Stalin Line" a well-fortified position behind their pre-war frontier, the recent seizure of Polish and Baltic territories meant that they had to meet the German onslaught well to the west of it, with the result that the Line's carefully-prepared defences were of little use. Even in the first week, the Soviet army suffered staggering losses, and the government faced the appalling task of organising defences, virtually from scratch, when the invader was already advancing into the country at the rate of 20 miles a day.

By early September 1941 the first phase of the offensive was over. Helped in the north by the vengeful Finns, the Germans had Leningrad completely surrounded: from there the line ran southwards through Smolensk and Dnepropetrovsk towards the Crimea. In a single brilliant encirclement east of Kiev, the 1st and 2nd Panzer groups claimed 665,000 prisoners, and altogether the German forces had captured well over one million Russian soldiers, largely because they insisted on fighting where they stood.

At this point Hitler intervened. For five vital weeks he vacillated before finally accepting his generals' original advice to concentrate on Moscow, rather than on the productive areas of the Ukraine and Donetz basin. The result was that although the renewed attack at the beginning of October soon resulted in the taking of a further 663,000 prisoners near Vyazma and Bryansk and in the capture of Kharkov and the Crimea to the south, it was now too late to take Moscow before the winter. To an army dependent on wheeled vehicles, the autumn mud was almost as severe a handicap as the winter cold. On December 5th, at one point only 15 miles from Moscow, the forward commanders Reinhardt and Guderian came to a halt.

Soviet Counter-Offensive (December 1941-May 1942)

Hitler's intervention had therefore saved the Russians from having to fight a possibly decisive battle in front of Moscow before they were ready for it. They made excellent use of the time thus granted them. Fresh forces were rushed from Siberia to the defence of the capital, and once the exhausted German army was halted the stage was set for a Soviet counter-offensive.

It is worth while considering what this meant in terms of human misery and superhuman effort. The Russians had already lost two-thirds of their pre-war coal-producing areas and three-quarters of their iron-ore production. Their armies had suffered over 4 million casualties, and 35 million of the population lived in what was now the German-occupied zone. Yet even while the rout of the Russian forces was going on, the Soviet government successfully dismantled whole

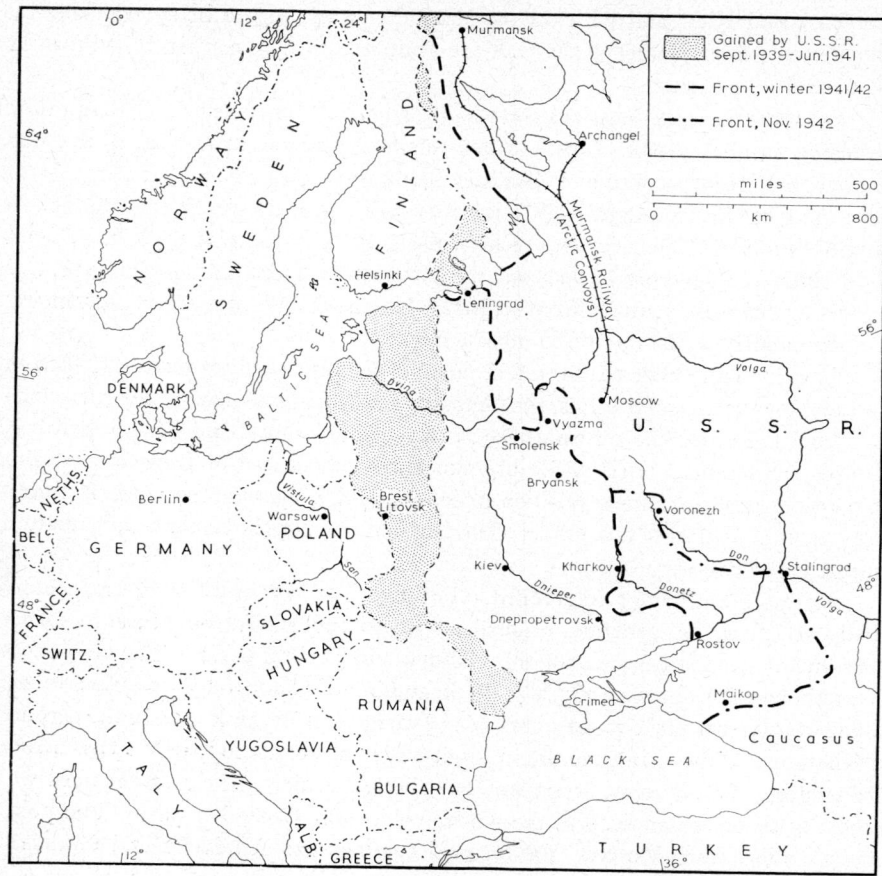

The Russian Front 1939-42

factories and moved them to the east, while simultaneously raising and equipping fresh armies. The fact was, that despite early warnings from their military attaché in Moscow, the Germans had greatly underestimated Russian manpower and industrial capacity. It was true that the British and Americans had responded generously to Stalin's appeal for assistance on July 3rd. It was also true that the Germans were obliged to maintain substantial forces elsewhere. Nevertheless, the real secret was Russian patriotism, a patriotism ready to accept the enormous sacrifices called for, to implement a "scorched earth" policy, to organise guerilla forces behind German lines. This was the force which one dictator spurned, but the other cultivated.

Hence the Russian counter-offensive was ready to begin just a day after the German advance was halted. For the first time, the Germans were caught on the wrong foot: having confidently anticipated a rapid victory, they were in no way

German infantry on the Eastern Front.
(Imperial War Museum)

prepared for winter operations. However, despite relieving the threat to Moscow, the efforts of the Soviet troops under Marshals Koniev, Zhukov, and Timoshenko were otherwise indecisive. The Russian armies as yet lacked the training and experience to take full advantage of the Germans' temporary weakness. Nevertheless, the offensive did have important effects: it demonstrated that the Germans could be beaten, enhanced the prestige of the Soviet government and the people's morale, and decided Hitler to take over as Commander-in-Chief of the German Army. This was followed by the retirement or dismissal of several German generals who did not share Hitler's faith in his own infallibility, a faith which was later to have tragic consequences for Germany.

German Advance on Stalingrad

For the time being, however, these consequences were not apparent, and in the summer of 1942 the Germans were able to launch another successful offensive, supported by Italy, Hungary and Rumania. Hitler was now in direct personal control. This time the chief target was the main Russian oilfields, situated in the Caucausus region to the south east. However, to protect the left flank of this assault it would also be necessary to capture Stalingrad, dominating the narrow neck of land between the Volga and the Don. Oil was essential to both armies, and Hitler expected the Russians to sacrifice their remaining manpower in the forthcoming battle.

At first everything went according to plan. Brushing aside an attempted Soviet offensive around Kharkov, the old Army Group South, now divided into Army Groups "A" and "B" under Field-Marshals List and von Bock, launched the familiar series of converging attacks. Voronezh fell on July 6th, Rostov on July 23rd, and German forces rapidly reached the oilfields and closed in on Stalingrad.

Nevertheless, all was not well. Contrary to German expectations, the offensive had not yielded large numbers of Russian prisoners; since 1941 Marshal Timoshenko had learned how to extricate the bulk of his forces, and far from having exhausted their human resources, the Russians still had over a million more trained men available than the Germans and their allies. Moreover, the vast distances involved were beginning to tell against the invaders and their vehicles. To their horror they found the oilfield at Naikop completely destroyed, and lorries bringing fuel to the front line used almost as much as they could carry on the journey itself. The Germans were strung out thinly, with perilously long supply lines, and an exposed flank to the north wide open to a Russian counter-attack. Hitler's typical reaction was to sack List and Halder, the chief of the Army General Staff, but there was no concealing the fact that his position was now vulnerable indeed.

"GREATER EAST ASIA CO=PROSPERITY SPHERE"

Japan and the West

Recent events in Europe had been watched with interest from the other side of the world by Japan. Alone among Asian countries, Japan was modern and highly industrialised, and for years had been seeking to expand beyond her native islands. In 1931 she had defied the League of Nations by seizing Manchuria from the Chinese; in 1937 she had begun a full-scale invasion of China which was still going on and which the U.S.A. had watched with growing anxiety. The Japanese made no secret of their belief that it was Japan's destiny to dominate eastern Asia, nor did it escape their notice that western powers with interests of their own in the area were no longer well-placed to defend them.

To the Japanese, heavily dependent on the U.S.A. for oil and raw materials, these European assets in the East were a standing temptation. Around the shores and among the islands of south-east Asia the French, Dutch, British and Americans controlled enormous natural wealth, much of it acquired long ago by conquests of dubious morality. What more natural, therefore, than that Japan, coveting those same assets, should proclaim a policy of Asia for the Asians, and prepare to put it into effect? In September 1940 Japan accordingly joined Italy and Germany in the Axis alliance, and by July 1941 pressure on the collaborationist (Vichy) government of France had enabled the Japanese to occupy French Indo-China. The Americans replied by demanding their withdrawal and placing an embargo on the supply of oil to Japan, an action which, in effect, offered the Japanese a choice between giving in and further easy conquests. Nevertheless negotiations began between the two powers in the hope of reaching a settlement.

The Japanese Prime Minister, General Tojo, however, believed that Japan's ambitions were certain to lead eventually to war against the U.S.A. and Britain and decided to strike a crippling blow first. Despite heavy commitments elsewhere, Japan could call on 11 divisions, about 1,150 aircraft, a powerful modern

27

navy, and adequate bases for attack.   Furthermore, she hoped to win at least the tacit support of native populations by declaring her aim to be the establishment of a "Greater East Asia Co-prosperity Sphere", which would end the bleeding of Asia for the benefit of Europeans.   By contrast, the Allies had widely-scattered possessions, no common defence plan, and total forces in the area greatly inferior to Japan's.

Pearl Harbour

The basic Japanese plan was to seize the richly-productive regions of south-east Asia, making Japan virtually self-sufficient for oil and raw materials, and then to protect their gains by establishing a defensive perimeter among the islands strong enough to deter the Allies from trying to dislodge them later.   The key to the success of this strategy was control of the sea and air, which would give the Japanese a marked advantage in the movement of troops and supplies.   It was

December 1941, *Pearl Harbour.   The great plume of smoke is from the battleship "Arizona".   (Imperial War Museum)*

therefore essential for Japan to destroy the Allies' sea and air forces as early and as suddenly as possible.

Accordingly, before any declaration of war, on December 7th 1941, 360 aircraft operating from fast aircraft carriers attacked the main base of the U.S. Pacific fleet at Pearl Harbour in the Hawaiian islands. The idea was copied by Admiral Yamamoto from the British success at Taranto, but the result was more spectacular. It was early on Sunday morning, and the unsuspecting Americans were taken completely by surprise: 2,400 lost their lives, 5 battleships were sunk or crippled, and over 200 aircraft destroyed on the ground. It was all over in an hour and a quarter. Simultaneously, the U.S. air base at Midway was heavily damaged, and in the next few days the garrisons at Guam and Wake Island were bombed and overwhelmed.

The War on the Mainland

The way was now clear for the main Japanese onslaught, a two-pronged attack with its greatest strength on the right. Six divisions would move against the British in Malaya and southern Burma; one strengthened division would seize Hong Kong; and $2\frac{1}{2}$ divisions would account for the Americans in the Philippines. Finally, the two prongs would converge on the weaker Dutch East Indies.

The British position in Hong Kong, attacked on December 8th (the same day as Pearl Harbour—the difference in date results from the International Date Line), was untenable from the first. Even so, Major-General Maltby's two weak brigades, with little artillery and no air support, held out for 17 days, until the Japanese captured the water supplies and further resistance became impossible. Meanwhile, a much more serious blow to British prestige was taking shape on the Malay peninsula, where Singapore formed the focal point of Britain's Far East defences. The danger of a Japanese attack there had been clear since July, but because of Churchill's overriding interest in the desert campaign little had been done to prepare for it. Instead of the great fleet necessary, Singapore held only the battleship *Prince of Wales* and the battlecruiser *Repulse*, plus a handful of cruisers and destroyers. Aircraft were few and old, unable to offer any protection to the fleet; but airfields had been built which must now be kept out of enemy hands, and that meant dangerous dispersal of ground forces.

Lt.-Gen. Percival, the Army commander, had nearly 90,000 men altogether, though of very mixed quality. He was opposed by smaller numbers of Japanese who, contrary to popular belief in Britain, were neither specially trained nor naturally suited for jungle warfare. But they had over 200 tanks to Percival's none, plus the support of more than 500 aircraft—and in those circumstances not even the fact that the Japanese plan conformed to British expectations could help the defenders much.

"Greater East Asia Co-prosperity Sphere"

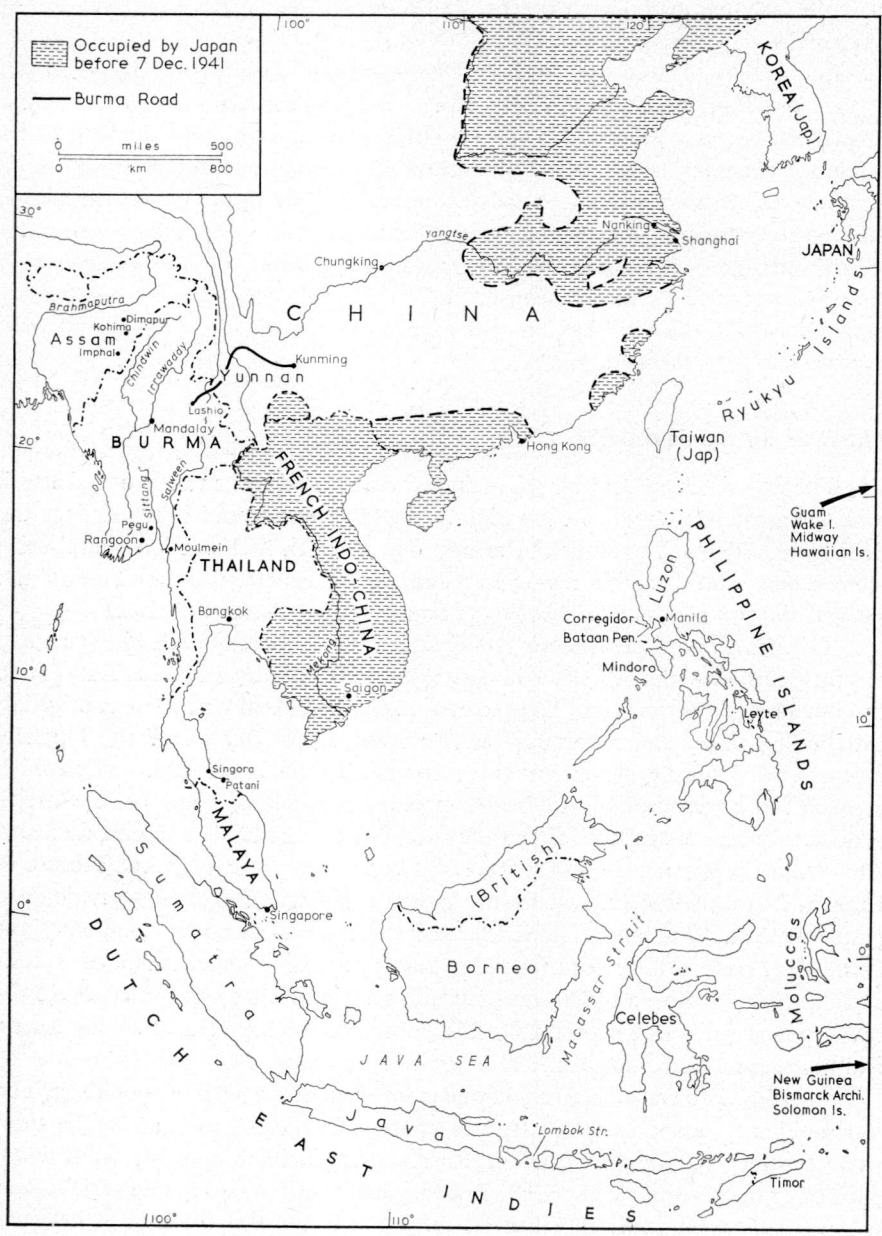

South East Asia 1941-42

"Greater East Asia Co-prosperity Sphere"

The onslaught began on December 8th with the seizure of Bangkok by the Japanese 25th Army under Lt.-Gen. Yamashita. Simultaneously, they landed two divisions at Singora and Patani in the extreme south of Thailand, and advanced into Malaya. The superiority of their "Zero" fighters rapidly assured them domination of the air, more than half the British planes being lost on the first day; and two days after that Japanese bombers from Saigon sank both *Prince of Wales* and *Repulse*, leaving the invaders in complete control of the sea. The defending troops were ill-trained, and continually outflanked by Japanese infiltration and fresh landings in their rear. Inevitably, by the end of January they had been driven from the peninsula and bottled up on Singapore itself. The island was

The Burma Campaign. Note the mule being used to carry baggage.
(*Imperial War Museum*)

"Banzai !" Japanese troops celebrate the capture of Christmas Island.
(Imperial War Museum)

strongly fortified on the seaward side, but defenceless from the rear, and reinforcements finally arrived just in time to surrender with the rest of the garrison on February 15th 1942.

Opinion in Britain was staggered by these disasters. Singapore had been widely regarded as one of the great fortresses of the Empire, yet it had been taken; worse still, it had fallen without a real fight; and worst of all (though not immediately realised) the 80,000 British prisoners taken there still greatly outnumbered the Japanese who had already humiliated them and were now to subject them to a barbaric captivity. Of all the many shocks sustained by Britain during the war, this was perhaps the worst.

Burma had also been invaded, on January 20th, by the Japanese 15th Army from Thailand. They were opposed at first by only two weak divisions of the Burma Army, and quickly took Moulmein, Pegu, and Rangoon. By that time, early March, two Chinese divisions had arrived to defend the Sittang valley, while the Burma Army under General Alexander held the valley of the Irrawaddy; but meanwhile the fall of Singapore enabled the Japanese to double their strength in

Burma. After that, all was soon over. The Japanese drove northwards towards Mandalay and cut the Burma Road (China's only land link with the West) at Lashio. The Burma Army was then obliged to withdraw across the Irrawaddy into India, on a march of great hardship during which they lost virtually all their heavy equipment.

The War in the Islands

While these events were taking place on the mainland, the left or eastern branch of the Japanese offensive was meeting similar success in the islands. General MacArthur, the American commander in the Philippines, controlled about 130,000 men, but most of them were reservists and only one-tenth were American. The Philippine group consists of over 7,000 islands, almost entirely dependent on imports for war materials: given the great naval predominance of the Japanese, therefore, the most that MacArthur could hope for was to hold out as long as possible on Luzon, the largest of the islands. The Japanese began with air-strikes on December 8th 1941 which destroyed nearly half of the American aircraft. Two days later the Japanese 14th Army, nearly 60,000 battle-seasoned troops under Lt.-Gen. Homma, began landing at both ends of the island, to converge on the capital at Manila. The defenders fought stubbornly, but at the end of a month they had been pushed back to the natural fortresses of the Bataan peninsula and the tiny island of Corregidor, cut off from all hope of relief.

The speed of Japanese successes on both flanks meant they were free to converge on the Dutch East Indies sooner than expected. There, the problems of defence were similar to those in the Philippines: a colossal army would be necessary for overall security, whereas the forces actually available were nearly all native troops of uncertain quality. As before, Allied warships and aircraft were greatly outnumbered, though the former gave a brave if hopeless account of themselves in actions in the Macassar and Lombok Straits, and in the Java Sea (January-February 1942). During January, the enemy landed in Borneo, Celebes and the Bismarck archipelago; in February came the assault on Java, Sumatra and the more southerly islands; and on March 9th the Dutch surrendered their possessions to Japan. All this time, Bataan and Corregidor, the only positions to offer any real resistance to the invaders, had held out and even inflicted reverses on the enemy, despite starvation and disease. Now they could do no more, and on May 6th the last American forces in the Philippines also capitulated. The Japanese, who occupied parts of New Guinea and the Solomon Islands besides, had thus established their defensive perimeter: but they were not to enjoy their triumph for long.

"LOOK FOR THE SILVER LINING"

In 1940 a French general declared that Britain would have her neck wrung like a chicken; but by mid-1942 it was the enemy's chickens which were coming home to roost. Before that year was out, victories at Alamein, Stalingrad and Midway had marked the turning-point in the war. Even at the end of 1941 the British 8th Army, under the new Commander-in-Chief Middle East, Sir Claude Auchinleck, had relieved Tobruk and driven Rommel from Cyrenaica in "Operation Crusader". This was the first British victory of the war over German troops. Moreover, considerable numbers of men from enemy-occupied countries had found their way into fighting units such as General De Gaulle's Free French, while Britain was also host to several Governments-in-Exile, keeping alive the hope and broadcasting the determination of their people to resist and ultimately to conquer.

Still more significant were the effects of the Japanese attack on Pearl Harbour. The immediate result was war between Japan and the U.S.A.: it was by no means certain that the U.S.A. would also declare war on Germany. In the event President Roosevelt had no choice, for on December 11th, 1941, Hitler declared war on the U.S.A. in support of his ally. In this way he unnecessarily added to his enemies and the balance of power began to swing emphatically against the Axis. In the long run, they had to contend with the almost unlimited industrial potential of the U.S.A., besides the apparently inexhaustible manpower of the U.S.S.R.

Meanwhile, the essential co-ordination of the Allied effort developed steadily. Even while the U.S.A. was still technically neutral, this process had begun. Roosevelt and Churchill had already met on board ship off Newfoundland, and produced a joint statement of their war aims in the Atlantic Charter (June 1941). This affirmed support for nations' right of self-determination, and condemned the aggressors. It was followed in January 1942 by the Declaration of the United Nations, in which all the major Allies and 21 other countries subscribed to the principles of the Atlantic Charter, and pledged themselves to make no separate

Rommel (Imperial War Museum)

peace with the enemy. Simultaneously, British and American military leaders, meeting in Washington at the Arcadia Conference, began joint planning for the defeat of Germany which Roosevelt now insisted for strategic reasons must take priority over the war against Japan, and created the Combined Chiefs of Staff Committee to advise their two governments. Its most prominent members were the American General George Marshall and the British General Sir Alan Brooke. Differences over details of strategy of course remained; but there is no doubt that these meetings laid the essential foundations not only for victory in the war, but also for the United Nations Organisation of later years.

The End in the Desert

The British, however, had first to receive a sharp lesson from General Rommel. A vital feature of the desert war was the problem of supply and maintenance: everything the armies needed had first to be brought into the country, and then transported across the arid, featureless landscape to the front by lorry. This put a premium on control of the sea, and meant that the further an army moved from its base, and the more its vehicles broke down under the strain, the weaker it became—while its enemy, falling back nearer and nearer to its own base, grew relatively stronger. This principle was about to be demonstrated in both directions.

Auchinleck's "Crusader" offensive had taken a heavy toll of British tanks, and confirmed that the equipment and professional standards of the "Desert Rats"—despite their superior numbers—were not yet a match for the German "Afrika Korps". Moreover, the problem of naval and air support had become acute. Since the losses in Crete, Admiral Cunningham's fleet had been out-gunned 3 to 1 by the Italians, the carrier *Ark Royal* had been sunk, and a daring raid by Italian frogmen on Alexandria harbour had damaged other ships. In December, Japan's entry into the war made necessary the withdrawal of aircraft for the Far East, while Rommel was at last receiving satisfactory ground and air reinforcement.

In January 1942 Auchinleck, therefore, withdrew to a line between Gazala and Bir Hacheim, which Rommel attacked in strength on May 27th. The enemy's use of mixed groups of armour, infantry, and artillery who had been carefully trained together, meant that despite being outnumbered in tanks by well over 3 to 1, he was able in little more than a month to inflict a crushing defeat on the 8th Army. This time, Tobruk fell and Rommel's forces raced into Egypt. In July they were halted by Auchinleck in a protracted action at El Alamein, only 60 miles from Alexandria (this was the first and less famous battle of El Alamein). However, Rommel himself was now in difficulties. His long advance had left him short of petrol, troops, and tanks, but he was compelled to gamble everything on a last attempt to break through to the Nile. Meanwhile, the British had made changes again. In August, Auchinleck was succeeded as Commander-in-Chief by General Alexander from Burma, and the 8th Army itself was taken over by Lt.-Gen. Montgomery. The latter, recognising the deficiencies of his force in a mobile battle, determined to let Rommel come to him in prepared defensive positions, and the result was an action at Alam Halfa (September 1942) which halted Rommel's advance for good.

The 8th Army was massively re-equipped with American vehicles and aircraft, but despite great pressure from Churchill, the methodical Montgomery refused to take the offensive until his men were adequately prepared. By October 23rd he was ready, and at El Alamein a prolonged slogging-match ended with Rommel in full retreat across 1,500 miles of desert, eluding his pursuers with tremendous skill. Four days later the fresh Anglo-American 1st Army under the American General Eisenhower landed in the Germans' rear at Algiers, Oran, and Casablanca, thus catching the enemy in Tunisia between Eisenhower and Montgomery. Nevertheless, there was a faint possibility that these new Allied forces could be defeated

October 1942. *British infantry in the dust of desert battle.*
(*Imperial War Museum*)

before Montgomery was able to arrive, and this persuaded Hitler to send in substantial reinforcements. The move did thwart Allied hopes of taking Tunis by Christmas, but in the long run, as Allied naval and air strength built up, it merely meant that larger numbers of Germans were trapped. In May 1943 they surrendered. Rommel himself escaped, but this unnecessary loss of 200,000 seasoned troops greatly facilitated the Allies' re-entry into Europe two months later.

Stalingrad

Meanwhile, Germany's main field armies were locked in battle with the Russians at Stalingrad. Here they were held for two months of bitter house-to-house fighting by the Soviet 62nd Army under General Chuikov. Failure on the Volga might well have resulted in a major collapse of Russian morale, but they had learnt a lot since their early defeats, and by mid-November 1942 the able and imaginative Zhukov was ready to counter-attack with no less than 12 armies. On November 19th-20th, under the command of Generals Rokossovski and Yeremenko, they struck north and south of the city, and 250,000 men of the enemy's 4th and 6th Armies were rapidly encircled.

A German break-out to the rear was still possible, but Hitler insisted they should hold their positions, though by now the forces on their flanks—largely Rumanian and Italian—were crumbling rapidly, and disaster seemed imminent. In January the Russians advanced on Rostov, threatening to cut off the 400,000 Germans of Kleist's Army Group "A" in the Caucasus. Thanks partly to their compatriots' resistance at Stalingrad, they narrowly escaped nonetheless. But nothing could save the Germans in the pocket at Stalingrad itself. On January 31st, frozen and starving, they surrendered, their commander von Paulus earning the dubious distinction of becoming the first German Field-Marshal ever to be captured. The effect on German morale was immense: after Stalingrad, Hitler's leadership lost its magic.

The Pacific

In the Pacific, by contrast, seapower was the decisive factor. An essential part of the Japanese war plans had been the destruction of the American fleet at Pearl Harbour, for Japan, like Britain, depended on merchant shipping to carry essential supplies to the homeland and maintain her forces overseas. However, Pearl Harbour had not been the devastating blow to the Americans that it originally seemed, and indeed might have been. To begin with, the Japanese had failed to destroy the oil tanks, without which the Americans would have had to withdraw to the U.S.A. Moreover, there had been no aircraft carriers at Pearl Harbour, and the destruction of the battleships there merely settled an old argument in U.S. Navy circles, and decided them to plan their future tactics round the carriers. It was Japan's turn to be taken by surprise.

"Look For the Silver Lining"

In March 1942 the Allies agreed that the Americans should assume responsibility for the Pacific theatre of war. General Douglas MacArthur and Admiral Chester Nimitz, both energetic leaders with more than their share of individualism, were placed in command. The Americans had broken the Japanese secret code, and learned in May that the enemy planned a naval thrust southwards to occupy Port Moresby in New Guinea, as the beginning of a scheme to block the sea-routes between America and Australia. U.S. forces under Rear-Admiral Fletcher sailed to intercept them, and the result was the battle of the Coral Sea, the first engagement ever between carrier fleets, at ranges of over 100 miles. Losses were about even—but the Japanese abandoned their objective.

Worse was to follow for Japan. The Americans soon heard via the Japanese code that the enemy also planned an assault on Midway Island (June 1942) in the hope of drawing the U.S. fleet into action and finishing it off. Admiral Yamamoto's total force for this expedition included four large carriers, seven battleships and ten heavy cruisers. Nimitz could muster only three carriers and seven heavy cruisers, under Admirals Spruance and Fletcher. However, their earlier successes had left the Japanese over-confident, and they made the mistake of dividing their forces, thus enabling the Americans to concentrate their attack on the main carrier fleet commanded by Admiral Nagumo. This time the American dive-bombers, catching their enemy in the act of rearming his own planes, decided the issue. All four Japanese carriers and their aircraft were sunk, for the loss on the American side of the carrier *Yorktown*. The enemy's continued superiority in battleships and cruisers was of comparatively little account, since these vessels would now be too dependent on protection by land-based aircraft. Midway thus reversed Pearl Harbour.

Nevertheless, the Japanese did not immediately abandon their offensive plans, but turned to the construction of a major air-base on Guadalcanal in the Solomon Islands. The result was a six-month struggle for the island between U.S. marines and Japanese troops, which ended in the latter's withdrawal in February 1943 after losing 25,000 men. Significantly, the decisive factor in this second setback was American superiority in a series of naval actions in which, though both fleets suffered badly, Japanese losses of pilots and aircraft were much the more severe. Meanwhile, a Japanese attack against Port Moresby by land was also heavily defeated.

Atlantic Trade and Arctic Convoys

In the Atlantic, too, the struggle was prolonged. The Allies' chief priorities there were to build up sufficient imports of food and materials into Britain to provide for her own needs and for future landings in Europe, and also to supply the Russians with aid via the Arctic Ocean. Hitler ordered the renewal of the "Battle of the Atlantic" in February 1941: his weapons were the U-boat, the

A convoy in the Channel (Radio Times Hulton Picture Library)

surface raider, and the Luftwaffe. At the time, however, Germany had only 21 submarines fit for such service, and only about a dozen "Kondor" aircraft capable of flying as far as 20° W. The British, by contrast, were soon able with help from Canada and "neutral" U.S.A. to provide escorts for convoys of merchantmen across the whole width of the North Atlantic, so that by the summer shipping losses were down, stocks of food and materials were up, and the *Bismarck* action (May 1941) had crippled the German surface vessels.

Undeterred, the enemy built up his forces dramatically, and by the beginning of 1942 Admiral Dönitz had 90 U-boats ready for action and another 250 on the stocks. German long-range bombers had meanwhile become an even greater danger than the submarines. Moreover, with the battleship *Tirpitz* as his flagship, Grand-Admiral Raeder had assembled in Norwegian waters a force ready to prey on the Allied Arctic convoys.   The threat offered by these raiders is best illustrated by the story of Convoy PQ 17 (June 1942).   Ordered to scatter when it seemed likely that *Tirpitz* would attack, PQ 17 lost 25 of her 36 merchantmen to the Luftwaffe and the U-boats.   Meanwhile, in the mid-Atlantic, beyond the range of Allied air cover, U-boats hunting in packs on the surface were inflicting losses nearly twice as heavy as in 1941, and seriously endangering the Allies' war plans. Losses were also very severe off the American coast, where a "wartime mentality" took time to develop.

There was no easy solution.   To concentrate on building escort vessels would mean reducing the output of cargo ships to replace losses, and of assault craft for future offensives.   Bombing of German industry, though advocated by the British Air Staff even to the extent of transferring aircraft from anti-submarine duties, proved singularly ineffective.   During 1942 the American 8th Air Force arrived in Britain to join the R.A.F. in such attacks, but Germany's industrial production rose by 80% despite more accurate bombing, and the U-boats themselves were unscathed.   The fact was that really effective bombing would not be possible until the Allies held command of the air, which was far from being the case at that time. Nevertheless, the Allies' greater resources told in the end.   Victory came in spring 1943 when Admiral Horton, an ex-submariner now commanding in the Western Approaches, decided to employ some of his increasing number of escorts in a counter-attack role.   In successive trials of strength during April and May, the U-boats suffered heavy losses and were withdrawn from the battle.

This victory was soon to make possible large-scale American participation in the war in Europe and increasingly massive aid to Russia.   Even at the Casablanca conference in January 1943, Churchill and Roosevelt felt able to declare that they would settle for nothing less than "unconditional surrender by Germany, Italy, and Japan"—a decision which, as it happened, almost certainly helped to prolong the war by stiffening the enemy's determination to fight on.   At the time, however, optimism prevailed as the Allied leaders planned their return to "fortress Europe".

DECLINE AND FALL

The Italian Surrender

At Casablanca, the Allies decided first to invade Sicily in order to control the sea passage between the western and eastern Mediterranean. The task was assigned to General Alexander's 15th Army Group, and on July 10th 1943 the American 7th and British 8th Armies landed from the sea and air alike along the southern coasts of the island. Thanks partly to Hitler's failure to withdraw Rommel's veterans from Tunisia in time, and partly to clever Allied deception of the Germans' intelligence services, resistance was comparatively light, and large numbers of Italians were taken prisoner. However, most of the German defenders were allowed to escape across the Straits of Messina, the first link in what was to become a chain of missed opportunities.

Meanwhile, these events had had important repercussions in Italy itself. On July 25th, Mussolini was deposed and succeeded by Marshal Badoglio, who promptly asked for an armistice. This request caught the Allies unprepared. They had made no firm plans for an invasion of Italy, partly because they were already committed to large-scale landings in France the following year. The Germans, by contrast, had anticipated the Italian collapse, and were ready to seize control of the country by the time the armistice was eventually signed on September 3rd. Meanwhile, a mixed British/American force of some 11 divisions began landing on the Italian mainland at Reggio, Taranto, and Salerno. But the Allies had lost the chance to exploit their unexpected good fortune by taking Rome and the whole of southern Italy. Their aim was simply to capture airfields needed to bomb new targets like the Rumanian oil wells, and to tie down German forces which might otherwise help to prevent the invasion of France. At Salerno, where a German Panzer division was stationed, resistance was stiff, but elsewhere the Allied advance was needlessly cautious; three weeks passed before Naples and the airfields around Foggia were taken. By then Sardinia and Corsica had also fallen and the Italian fleet had surrendered to Admiral Cunningham at Malta—but with more daring much more might have been achieved.

The Russian Front, 1943

In the East, too, though the Germans had suffered a severe setback at Stalingrad, they were by no means beaten. In a masterly performance during February and March 1943, Manstein's Panzers of Army Group South had turned back the advancing Soviet armies west of Kharkov and regained the line of the Donetz river. The long retreat from Stalingrad and the Caucasus had shortened the German front and thus created surplus strength. Moreover, new and superior "Tiger" and "Panther" tanks were now being produced in quantity under Guderian's supervision, and Hitler decided on a massive attack to restore the confidence of his troops—"Operation Citadel".

Around the town of Kursk the Russians held a huge salient, or bulge, flanked by German forces to north and south. Hitler aimed to nip off this bulge by striking towards Kursk from both directions with no less than 2,700 tanks. This was as many tanks as the whole German army had possessed in 1940, but a six-week delay to await their production meant that when the attack came on July 5th the Russians were ready for it. In the skies overhead the Luftwaffe no longer enjoyed its accustomed superiority, and in the first week the Germans advanced only 9 miles. Then the Russians counter-attacked, and the opposing armour clashed head-on in the greatest tank battle of the war, just when the invasion of Sicily compelled Hitler to withdraw troops from the East to defend Italy and the Balkans. The battle for Kursk cost the Germans 2,000 tanks and 70,000 men, and when it ended they were in retreat once more.

Ironically enough, a planned withdrawal by the Germans in the spring might well have drawn the Russians into a trap and exposed them to a shattering counterstroke. Hitler, however, refused to consider a withdrawal then, and now the forces which might have delivered the counter-blow had been smashed in the salient at Kursk. Consequently, during the autumn of 1943 the Soviet offensive rolled relentlessly forward along a 600-mile front. Too weak to resist effectively, the Germans fell back under constant artillery bombardment from the Donetz to the Dnieper, an immensely strong natural defence line which nevertheless they failed to hold. They lost the richest areas they had captured in Russia and their 17th Army was cut off in the Crimea. Kursk had been decisive.

The Teheran Conference

It was against this background of victories that the so-called "Big Three" (Churchill, Roosevelt and Stalin) met for the first time at Teheran in November 1943. The meeting took place essentially in an attempt to iron out differences between them, which were starting to appear now that final victory seemed certain, and the problem of a post-war settlement for Europe was beginning to raise its head.

A particularly sensitive question had recently arisen. The Germans had discovered at Katyn, near Smolensk, the bodies of some 4,000 Polish officer

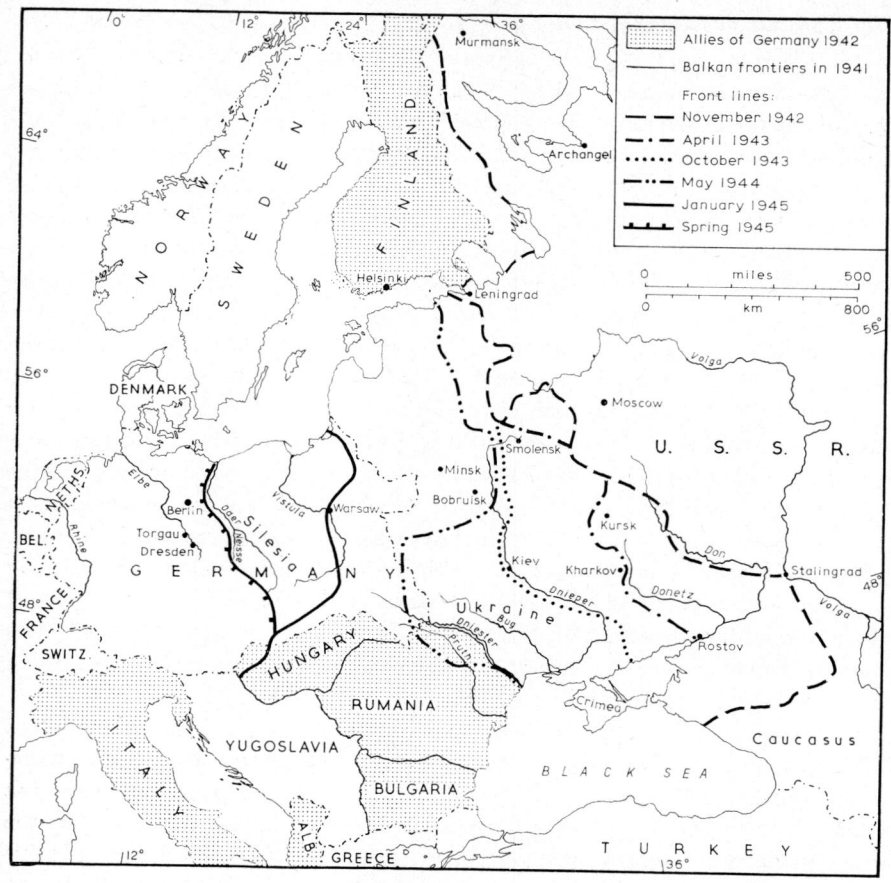

The Russian Front 1942-45

prisoners, apparently shot by the Russians in 1940. The exiled Polish leaders in London demanded an enquiry, which the Russians refused, and the suspicion grew that Stalin was preparing to impose a puppet government of his own supporters on Poland as soon as the opportunity presented itself.

Churchill had no wish to see a post-war Europe in which German domination was simply replaced by that of Russia, and partly for that reason he advocated a campaign by the western Allies in the Balkans, which he felt would bring both military and political dividends. The Germans certainly feared such a development. The Americans, though, regarded the Balkans as a blind alley, and suspected that Churchill was not as wholeheartedly behind the proposed invasion of France as they would wish. Stalin, who had no desire to see a British/American presence in south-east Europe which might obstruct his own very different plans for the future of those countries, backed the American view. Churchill was not prepared to risk a breach with the Americans, and at Teheran Roosevelt seemed determined to adopt a policy of "Hear no evil, see no evil, speak no evil", as far as Stalin was concerned. Even Churchill was mollified by a Soviet offer to join the war against Japan once Germany was defeated. The result was that the Katyn affair was brushed aside, the Balkan idea dropped, and the Russians assured that the invasion of France would receive top priority. Stalin thus gained a major diplomatic victory to add to his military successes.

The Russian Advance (Spring 1944)

In 1943, Hitler, by refusing to withdraw in time, had sacrificed much of his strength on the eastern front. Consequently, when the Russians opened their next offensive at the beginning of 1944 they outnumbered the Germans almost 2 to 1 in men, and overwhelmingly in tanks and artillery. Furthermore, the early months of 1944 were unusually mild and the front was soon a sea of mud. This, too, was to the Russians' advantage. Their tanks had wider tracks than the German ones and ran better in the muddy conditions. They were also well supplied with four-wheel-drive American trucks which kept going when German vehicles were hopelessly bogged down.

Inevitably, more German defeats swiftly followed. In January, Leningrad was relieved at last after a two-and-a-half year siege during which nearly a million people had died of starvation. Further south, the German line in the Ukraine crumbled before the onslaught of three Soviet "Fronts" (Army Groups) under Zhukov. From one river-line to the next—Bug, Dniester, Pruth—the Germans were forced back. In May, the Crimea fell. With an invasion of France imminently expected, Hitler could not send reinforcements. What he did do was characteristic: he sacked his generals, Manstein and Kleist.

The Struggle for Italy

In Italy, too, there had been changes in command. Eisenhower and Montgomery returned to Britain to prepare for the invasion of France, leaving Alexander as Commander-in-Chief of Land Forces with orders to tie down the maximum number of German troops. Meanwhile, the Germans—unaware that the Allies had failed to agree on positive action in the Balkans, but persuaded by their own assessment of its possibilities that such an operation was likely—obligingly trebled their strength in Italy to 25 divisions under Field-Marshal Kesselring, with a further 24 in south-east Europe. However, another opportunity for the Allies was about to slip away.

1944, *The Battle of Cassino. Men of the Fifth Army searching for snipers* (*Imperial War Museum*)

At the beginning of 1944 the Germans held a strong position known as the "Gustav Line", running along the Sangro and Garigliano rivers. The keystone of this position was the ancient monastery of Monte Cassino, and, although the Americans argued in favour of husbanding resources for use in France, it was eventually decided to launch an assault on Monte Cassino to coincide with a landing in the enemy's rear near Rome. On January 22nd 50,000 Allied troops went ashore at Anzio. They were initially opposed by only one battalion of Germans, but the American commander was pessimistic about breaking out from his beach-head and simply stayed put while Kesselring brought up powerful reinforcements. Meanwhile, the attacks on Monte Cassino were proving difficult and costly. The mountainous country and the destruction caused by bombing made tanks useless; mules were the universal transport. In the most international battle of the war, with troops of 15 nations involved, it took four months and four major attacks before Polish forces finally captured the monastery hill on May 18th. Rome was not entered until June 4th, nearly a year after the landing in Sicily.

Decline and Fall

From the first, Allied operations in Italy had been inhibited by disagreements as to the relative importance of the area and the initial emphasis on passive tactics. Now, immediately before the invasion of France, they had certainly achieved their aim of "holding down" strong enemy forces, but it had been a disappointing year nevertheless—not least for the people of the occupied countries still waiting to be freed from oppression.

OCCUPIED EUROPE

When Mr Chamberlain told the nation in his broadcast on the outbreak of war with Germany, "It is evil things we shall be fighting against", few in Britain really had much idea how true his words would turn out to be. Of course, Hitler's anti-Jewish views were well known, but they were at least partly shared by many Britons. There were rumours of concentration camps, but hardly anyone envisaged their real purpose. Mr Chamberlain spoke rather vaguely of "bad men" and "bad faith" and not until near the end did the victors learn the truth about the horrors of Nazi methods.

Europe's Jews were the chief, though not the only, victims. Hitler had devised what he termed "the Final Solution" for the Jewish problem. It amounted to no less than a plan for the systematic extermination of European Jewry, and the names of Belsen, Dachau, Auschwitz, and many other concentration camps will long remain as an obscene memorial to Nazi "achievement". In them perished literally millions of Jews, Communists, Socialists and other groups designated as sub-human by the Nazi theorists of the *Herrenvolk*. The victims were starved, shot, gassed, even used as human guinea-pigs in so-called medical research. Women and children suffered equally with men. Sometimes it proved simpler to slaughter on the spot rather than going to the trouble of transporting the sufferers to camps: a notorious example was the massacre of 100,000 Jews in the ravine of Babi-Yar, outside Kiev in Russia. When all this was revealed, people were torn between horror at the enormity of the crime and awe at its sheer magnitude.

Another aspect of the Nazi order was the employment of slave labour on a hitherto undreamed-of scale. Massive deportations of workers from all over Europe impoverished their own countries, but freed Germans for actual combat, and made an important contribution to Germany's war effort. Much of this would have been difficult without the acquiescence of puppet regimes in the occupied countries themselves. One thinks for instance of the tragic figure of Marshal Pétain in France, hero of the defence of Verdun in the First World War and convicted traitor after the Second World War, of whom it was said, "He cared too much for the French people and too little for France". In eastern Europe, Bulgaria and Rumania had Nazi-style governments and were allies of Germany, until they were forced to change sides by the advance of the Russians in 1944. Hungary was also a German ally, though not as subservient as Hitler wished until Admiral Horthy was overthrown in 1944 and a Nazi puppet government set up.

These nightmarish events were the inevitable product of the "master-race" philosophy and the Nazi party machine. Early in his political career Hitler had created, for the furtherance of Nazi policy and his own protection, a number of Party organisations such as the "S.S." (*Schutzstaffeln*) and "S.D." (*Sicherheitsdienst*). Except in Russia, where the German Army as a whole participated in atrocities, these forces bore the main responsibility for Nazi crimes. Led by depraved men like Heinrich Himmler, they were chosen for their dedication to Party "ideals", and were virtually private armies, quite distinct from the German Army proper—though they did provide *Waffen S.S.* units which fought alongside it. There was also the notorious Gestapo (*Geheime Staatspolizei*), which was a secret police organisation designed to root out opposition to the Führer. Men and women alike soon learned to dread the knock on the door in the small hours, and the brutal interrogation which inevitably followed, more than the firing-squad which for many came at last as a blessed release.

These methods naturally provoked considerable underground resistance, much of it inspired by the political left-wing. Long before the war, there were rival factions of left and right in most European countries: the Spanish Civil War provides the supreme example. Since the right-wing in many countries preferred the Nazis to political opponents of their own nationality, it was to be expected that much of the resistance would be organised by the (usually Communist) left. The Russians themselves claimed to have 600,000 men behind enemy lines in occupied Russia. In the West, Marshal Tito's Yugoslav partisans are perhaps better known. France and Italy, both countries with large Communist parties, also saw widespread guerilla activities. Their first object was, of course, to assist in the defeat of Hitler, but they also aimed at the establishment of sympathetic governments in their countries once that was achieved. Sometimes they failed, as happened in Greece, but elsewhere they were successful. The pro-Western Polish leaders in London, for example, could hardly compete against their Communist counterparts, who were soon to re-enter Poland in the wake of the Russian armies.

However, every occupied country had its share of resistance and reprisal, and it would be quite wrong to suppose that political allegiance was always a more important motive than simple patriotism. Indeed, the western Allies did all they could to encourage such movements; they supplied weapons, radio operators and other specialists, trained by the British Special Operations Executive or the American Office of Strategic Services, and these contributed materially to the eventual defeat of Germany. The BBC broadcast daily to occupied Europe, and the opening notes of Beethoven's 5th Symphony, spelling out the Morse Code sign "V" for Victory, came to symbolise hope for millions of oppressed people.

"D-day" 6 June 1944. Troops assembling on the beach from landing craft in the background. (Imperial War Museum)

"OVERLORD"

"D-Day"

The day after the fall of Rome a spate of such broadcasts heralded the long-awaited invasion of France. Appropriately code-named "Overlord", it was to be the greatest amphibious operation in the history of warfare, involving three airborne and five conventional divisions with nearly 7,000 vessels. For months beforehand much of England's south coast became a military training area closed to civilian visitors. Ports filled up with the armada of all kinds of craft which the invasion would require. For hundreds of miles roads were lined with the invaders' vehicles, which were to give the Allied armies a hitherto undreamt-of mobility. Since most of this material came from the U.S.A.—one American shipyard, for example, launched a ship a day for six months—it can be seen why victory over the U-boats in the Atlantic was so important. Without that, American participation on such a scale would have been impossible.

General Eisenhower was named as Supreme Allied Commander for the invasion, and he proved to be exactly fitted by temperament for the frequently trying task of co-ordinating the efforts of Allies who did not always see eye-to-eye. Air Chief Marshal Tedder was "Ike's" Deputy, in charge of air operations, while General Montgomery was to control all ground forces in the early stages. Their immediate opponent, responsible for defending the Channel coast with Army Group "B" (7th and 15th Armies), was Rommel. He had spent months strengthening his defences with mines, underwater obstacles and the like. However, the Allies had been busy, too. Tanks had been equipped with flails, to beat a path through Rommel's minefields; floating harbours ("Mulberries") had been built, ready to be towed across the Channel to provide landing facilities; a pipeline laid under the ocean ("PLUTO") would carry fuel to the beaches; and production of the long-range American "Mustang" fighters gave the Allies command of the air at the crucial moment. Lastly, in order to achieve surprise, plans had been made to deceive the enemy as to the precise spot chosen for the invasion, on the coast of Normandy between Caen and Cherbourg.

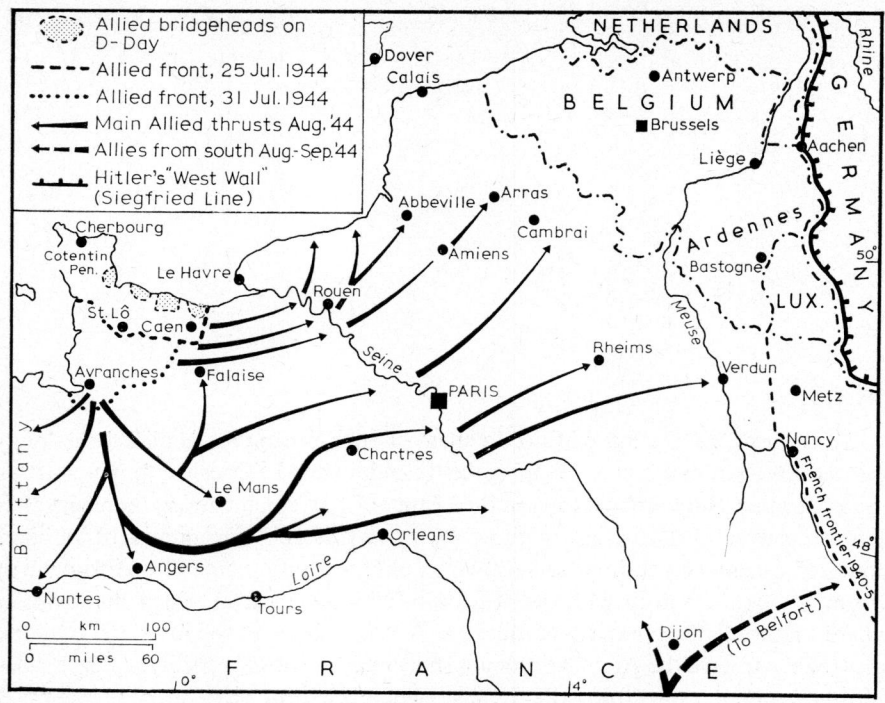

The Western Front 1944-45

June 6th 1944 has gone into history as "D-Day". The airborne divisions went first to protect the flanks of the seaborne assault, and by nightfall 156,000 Allied troops had landed, supported by overwhelming naval and air bombardment, and by sabotage from the French resistance. As it happened, Rommel was absent from the scene. Misled by unfavourable weather reports into supposing an invasion was unlikely for several days, he had gone home to Germany on a visit to Hitler. In fact, German reconnaissance had been so restricted by Allied air superiority that they remained ignorant of the imminence of the attack until it was upon them. Nevertheless, the invaders, particularly the American 1st and British 3rd divisions, met fierce resistance before darkness fell and found them in secure possession of their beach-heads.

The Breakthrough (July–September 1944)

The Germans now missed their only chance. The Commander-in-Chief West, von Rundstedt, had wanted a mobile armoured force available for counter-attack at the right time and place, but Hitler and Rommel disagreed. Rommel's experience in the desert had caused him to lose faith in such operations where the

Allies held command of the air, and he counted instead on using all his forces to stop the invaders on the beaches. Consequently, there was no substantial German counter-attack at first, and when reinforcements did arrive they had to be thrown into the battle piecemeal, rather than being husbanded for a major counterstroke. Moreover, Allied deception plans worked so well that long after the Normandy landings the German 15th Army—a good half of Rommel's available force—remained unused in the Pas de Calais, awaiting a second invasion which never came. Thus, for different reasons, both German commanders were quickly convinced the battle was lost, and were soon replaced.

Hitler's own reaction smacked of desperation. He urged his troops, now commanded by von Kluge, to stand fast until imminent new "miracle weapons"

June 1944. An American "Mulberry" harbour in Normandy allows heavy vehicles to be landed easily. (Imperial War Museum)

transformed the course of the war. But these so-called V (for "Vengeance") weapons—guided missiles released mainly on London from June 1944 to March 1945—proved to be of less than miraculous effect, and meanwhile the Allies steadily consolidated their foothold, taking Cherbourg on June 27th. There was still heavy fighting ahead, but the issue was no longer seriously in doubt. By July 1st the Allied build-up had put 27 divisions into France. It was true that the Germans still had more men on the ground than this, but in the air they were hopelessly outnumbered by over 12 to 1. This was part of the price Germany had to pay for becoming involved on two fronts simultaneously, and it meant that their troops and communications in the West would be subjected to virtually unhindered bombardment from the air whenever the weather was fine. Montgomery therefore looked forward confidently to the next stage of the battle. By continuous probing attacks, the British under General Dempsey on the Allied left would draw the bulk of the defenders towards them, in the area around Caen. This would leave General Bradley's Americans on the right facing comparatively weaker resistance, so that eventually they would break through, and the whole front would swing open like a door, with Caen as the hinge.

Despite widespread doubts, caused largely by the determined quality of the enemy resistance, this plan proved conspicuously successful. Dempsey's attacks around Caen attracted nearly all the German armour, including two divisions withdrawn from the eastern front, and most of the infantry reinforcements besides. Meanwhile, in the American sector, hard fighting among the hedgerows of the Cotentin peninsula secured St Lo and Avranches. By the end of July the enemy was on the verge of a spectacular collapse. A new character now took the stage in the figure of General Patton, commanding the U.S. 3rd Army. A flamboyant personality, celebrated equally for his cowboy-style gun belt and his lack of self-control, Patton quickly opened a gap on the coast and swung eastwards round the Germans' left flank. Simultaneously, the Canadian 1st Army broke southwards from Caen towards Falaise, where two German Panzer armies narrowly escaped encirclement. By August 25th most of Brittany was freed, the Allies had reached the Seine and Loire rivers, and Paris had fallen after a rising inside the city.

Meanwhile, Free-French and American armies had landed on August 15th in the south of France, which the Germans had occupied following the Allied invasion of Algeria in November 1942. Taking Lyons on September 3rd, they linked up with Eisenhower's forces near Dijon and drove the Germans before them towards the Vosges mountains and the Belfort gap. The British had opposed this move, partly because they thought it unnecessary, and partly because it meant withdrawing seven divisions from Italy. Nor had Churchill given up the idea of operations in the Balkans, despite the decisions taken at Teheran. That this fresh landing was unnecessary is suggested by the low level of resistance it encountered, and it certainly meant more long months of frustration on the Italian front, where the

*The Arnhem Landings, September 1944. Two sergeants of the Glider Pilot Regiment
search for snipers in the remains of a Dutch School.*
(Imperial War Museum)

reduced and disillusioned Allied forces were struggling at heavy cost to break through
Kesselring's Gothic Line north of Florence. However, for most people, the tide
of victory in the West washed all such thoughts away. Since D-Day the Germans
had suffered over a million casualties altogether, and although their general war
production was still increasing despite Allied bombing, they were already desperately short of oil. By mid-September, outnumbered 2 to 1, they stood at bay
with their backs to their own frontier.

The Struggle for the Rhine (September 1944-January 1945)

On September 1st Eisenhower took over operational command from Montgomery. The plan now was to advance into Germany on two fronts simultaneously,
north and south of the Ardennes, but the Allies had already outstripped their
supply organisation, and both Montgomery and Patton pleaded for the resources

*December 1944. German infantry at the Battle of the Bulge.
(Imperial War Museum)*

to make one concentrated thrust instead. Eisenhower knew that to favour either at the other's expense might cause trouble, so he rejected this idea. But Montgomery's attempt in mid-September to seize the bridge over the Rhine at Arnhem with airborne forces, and thus open the way to the North German Plain and Berlin, would probably have failed anyway. It was a bold plan, but too much of a gamble with the limited means available. The British 1st Airborne Division unluckily landed close to S.S. Panzer units whose presence in the area had been unsuspected, and the operation had eventually to be halted with the enemy still holding the north bank of the river. Another way into Germany would now have to be found. During the autumn Allied troops fought hard to break through Hitler's "West Wall", but the inevitable delay enabled him to assemble enough reserves to hit back. The Allies had missed their chance of victory in 1944.

By the turn of the year, however, Hitler's counterstroke had failed, too. He had planned to drive a wedge between the Allied armies with an offensive in the

Crossing the Rhine. U.S. paratroopers clearing the landing zone, while a British "Horsa" glider comes in to land (Imperial War Museum)

Ardennes, reminiscent of 1940, and this "Battle of the Bulge" might have resulted in two Panzer armies under Dietrich and von Manteuffel breaking out across the Meuse and threatening the vital port of Antwerp, only opened to Allied supplies in November after severe fighting. But the German armour had insufficient fuel to maintain its momentum, and the important road junction of Bastogne was stubbornly defended by an American airborne division under Brigadier-General McAuliffe. Moreover, the Americans reacted to the threat with remarkable speed. In a single day they poured in 60,000 fresh troops, and the Germans were repulsed. 1945 therefore opened with the snuffing-out of Hitler's last shot in the West, for which he had depleted his reserves and weakened his eastern front in fatal fashion.

German Collapse in the East (June-December 1944)

However, Hitler's last hope of stemming the Russian advance had already faded with his failure to defeat the invasion in Normandy. He was now irrevocably committed to facing virtually the whole military strength of the Soviet Union with not much more than half of his own. Hitler and his staff believed that Stalin's summer offensive for 1944 would be directed against their southern flank, where

Crossing the Rhine. U.S. paratroopers in a German orchard. Notice the parachute hanging from the tree. (Imperial War Museum)

the Russians had made such important gains in the spring, rather than against the centre where the Germans held their last extensive stretch of Soviet territory. Accordingly, they transferred to the southern flank the bulk of Army Group Centre's tanks. But to Soviet psychology, the freeing of Russian territory was much more important than purely strategic considerations—and it was on Army Group Centre that the blow fell.

On June 23rd the Russians attacked on a 450-mile front with four Army Groups, co-ordinated by Vassilevsky and Zhukov. Their total forces amounted to 160 divisions with thousands of tanks and aircraft, and the Germans' 38 divisions were simply overwhelmed. Ordered by Hitler to stand fast, hampered by shortage of transport and massive partisan attacks on their communications, the German defence collapsed as Russian units swept by on the flanks to cut off any escape at Minsk and Bobruisk. In less than a fortnight 25 German divisions were lost.

These victories were to lead to a cooling in relations between Russia and the Western Allies. On July 29th, when Russian troops had reached the outskirts of Warsaw, Moscow radio appealed to the Polish underground in the city to rise against the enemy. Led by General Bor-Komorowski, almost every able-bodied citizen responded at once, but the expected Russian help did not materialise, and the rising was crushed at the cost of 200,000 Polish lives. Though there were mitigating circumstances, it seemed to many that the Russians had deliberately encouraged the Polish underground movement to reveal itself, and had then stood callously by while it was destroyed. Coupled with the suspicions aroused by the Katyn massacre, and the fact that Moscow was now backing a Communist group as the next Polish government, the Warsaw affair made a Russian takeover in Poland appear imminent. To the British government especially, which had ostensibly gone to war to keep Poland free, this was a bitter pill to swallow. Moreover, during the autumn of 1944, as Russian troops swept forward into Rumania, Bulgaria and Hungary, those countries too seemed likely to become Communist satellites. Finland, however, was not occupied by the Russians—and Churchill at last had his way in Greece, too, by despatching a British force to forestall a Communist takeover there.

"THE JUNGLE IS NEUTRAL"

In the Far East the situation was less clear-cut than in Europe. Although the island part of Japan's empire had been put at risk by her naval/air defeats at Midway and Guadalcanal, on the mainland of Asia the Allies themselves faced enormous difficulties. Their only contact with China was by air, and that ruled out any early offensive against the main Japanese armies (which were stationed there), making it difficult even to send adequate help to the hard-pressed forces of Chiang Kai-Shek's inefficient government. Supply was also the chief problem on the frontier between Burma and India, where the Japanese had halted in 1942. It was wild country with no through roads or proper railways, and the only way across the great river Brahmaputra was by ferry—a threat to India from that quarter had never been envisaged. Months of work would be necessary before an attack could be mounted there. Finally, the Allies did not agree about priorities. The British naturally looked forward to the recapture of Malaya and the Dutch East Indies; the Americans, traditionally suspicious of colonial government, insisted that the liberation of China—or at least the re-opening of land communications—must come first.

The Road to Mandalay

In an attempt to solve at least some of these difficulties, a new South-East Asia command was set up in August 1943. The British Admiral Mountbatten was to be the Supreme Allied Commander, but his deputy was the notoriously quarrelsome American General "Vinegar Joe" Stilwell, who was also Chief-of-Staff to Chiang Kai-Shek, and could therefore be relied upon to look after American and Chinese interests. All agreed that it was desirable to launch offensives against the Japanese in Burma from India and China simultaneously, but the Chinese were reluctant to commit themselves until the supply problem had been solved.

Earlier in the year, however, something had occurred which changed the picture. Brigadier Orde Wingate, with 3,000 of his since-famous "Chindit" troops, had penetrated far behind the enemy front east of the Chindwin river in a raid which, though it proved costly, nevertheless had two important results. First, it demonstrated the feasibility of supplying forces in jungle country entirely by air; secondly, it persuaded the Japanese that their Chindwin front was insecure, and that they must attempt to forestall the expected Allied offensive by an attack of their own on the British bases in Assam—bases which were vital to the whole conception of an Allied campaign in Burma.

Thus it happened that the British 14th Army, long starved of supplies by the demands of other fronts and, in its own eyes, "forgotten" by the politicians at home, at last had its chance of immortality. Its commander, Lt.-Gen. Slim, had carefully studied the methods of infiltration which had brought the Japanese such success in their earlier campaigns, and had devised his own counter-tactics. He ordered his forces to fight where they stood, regardless of enemy infiltration around their flanks and rear. If surrounded, units would be supplied by air, thus creating strong points behind the attackers; Slim's mobile reserves would then close in. These tactics were to prove strikingly successful.

The main Japanese offensive was to be made by three divisions of their 15th Army under Lt.-Gen. Mutagachi. His plan was to seize the principal British positions at Imphal and Kohima by probing round their flanks, and then converging on them from north and south simultaneously. This would cut the British supply route from Dimapur and foil the Allies' plans for an offensive, but the difficult country created the same supply problems for the Japanese as it did for the British, with the difference that Mutagachi had neither the aircraft nor the reserves which Slim possessed. Moreover, such problems are normally greater for the attackers, and in this case they were heavily outnumbered by the defence. On this dubious note the offensive opened on February 4th 1944 with a diversionary attack in the province of Arakan. In the ensuing battle of the Ngakyedauk Pass, encircled troops of 7th Indian division were so efficiently supplied from the air that they were soon receiving daily deliveries of mail and newspapers, while their besiegers went hungry and ran short of ammunition—a bad omen for the main enemy assault on Imphal and Kohima, which furthermore began too late to derive any benefit from the diversion. Nevertheless, British dispositions were so unbalanced (Kohima being held by only 1,500 men) that Slim's troops needed all their determination before victory was theirs. The Japanese kept up the attack till they had suffered over 60% casualties, but early in July they fell back defeated to the Chindwin.

By then, however, their position between the Chindwin and the Irrawaddy was also under attack by Stilwell's Chinese divisions from the north, and a much-enlarged Wingate Special Force operating behind their lines. Moreover, Chiang Kai-Shek's forces, having held a Japanese offensive in central China, then managed to mount one of their own across the Salween from Yunnan. By January 1945 the Allies had succeeded in restoring the land-link with China along the Burma Road, and were threatening Mandalay from three directions. The most the Japanese could now hope for in this area was to hold on to the oil- and rice-producing regions of southern Burma, a slim hope at best.

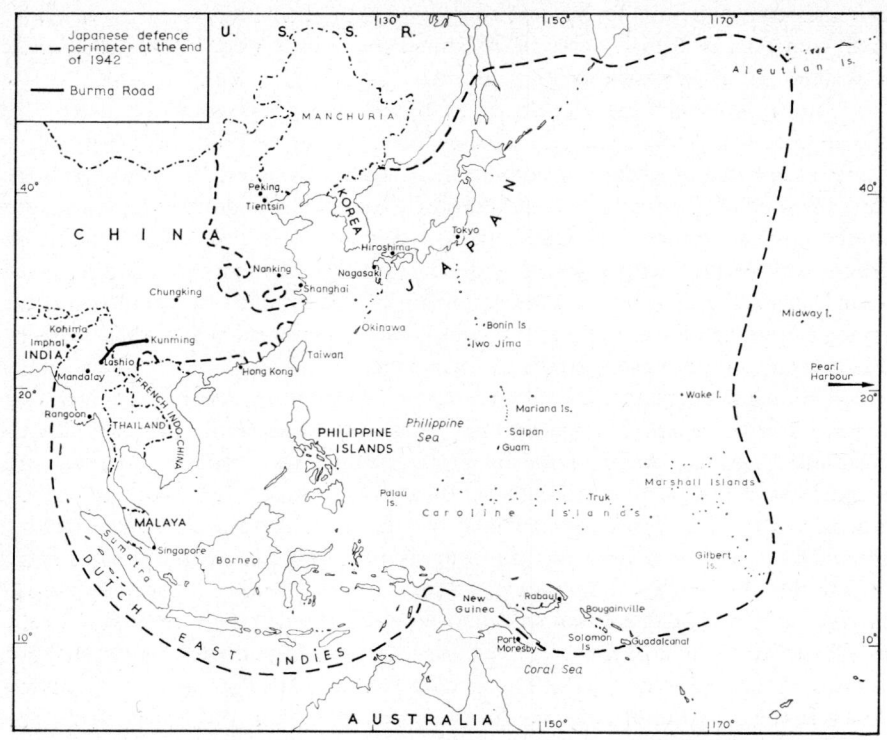

The Pacific Theatre of War 1942-45

Back to Bataan

A similar story had meanwhile been unfolding in the Pacific where the Allies had decided their main effort should be made, both in view of the difficulties they faced on the mainland, and the advantage they now possessed in sea- and air-power. Their plan was for two parallel thrusts. On the right, Admiral Nimitz would advance through the Gilbert, Marshall and Caroline Islands to the Marianas; meanwhile, General MacArthur on his left, with a smaller fleet but larger armies, would consolidate his hold on the Solomon Islands and New Guinea, before proceeding to the recapture of the Philippines.

However, despite increasingly worrying losses of merchant shipping to American submarines, the Japanese still believed towards the end of 1943 that they could win this kind of campaign. The islands were well-prepared and naturally suited to defence. Japan itself was out-of-range to existing bombers. By shortening their perimeter, the Japanese hoped to protect the vital raw materials of south-east Asia, and maintain seaborne communications within the area they would still control. To do this they were prepared to sacrifice the garrisons of their more distant outposts, and to take considerable risks with their fleet in the hope of reversing the American victory at Midway.

On land, the island-hopping campaign which followed was uniformly desperate and bloody, as isolated Japanese garrisons frequently threw their lives away rather than surrender. Nevertheless, the Americans, spearheaded by the Marines, could always concentrate superior forces: command of the sea and air and constantly increasing strength enabled them to dictate the pattern of the struggle, and to bypass Japanese strongpoints without endangering their own communications. Between November 1943 and February 1944 the Allies gradually reduced the enemy outposts, gaining valuable experience in amphibious operations on the way. Australians advanced along the coast of New Guinea, while Americans captured Bougainville. The important naval and air base at Rabaul in New Britain was cut off with its garrison of over 100,000 men. The Gilbert and Marshall Islands fell to overwhelming force, and the naval base at Truk in the Carolines was heavily raided by carrier aircraft.

In the light of these reverses the Japanese decided to strengthen their second line of defence in the Palau, Mariana and Bonin Islands. Thus, when the Americans landed three divisions on Saipan in the Marianas on June 15th 1944, the result was the great naval battle on which the Japanese counted to restore their fortunes—the battle of the Philippine Sea. Admiral Toyoda had a formidable fleet available, including five battleships and nine carriers. It was true that Admiral Spruance, commanding Nimitz's main battle fleet, had three times as many carriers, but Toyoda believed that land-based aircraft from Guam would level the odds. Accordingly, on the morning of June 19th, the Japanese carrier planes made four separate attacks on Spruance's carriers, losing two-thirds of their number to American fighters in the process. Meanwhile, American bombers had attacked the enemy airfields on Guam, crippling the force on which Toyoda had placed such reliance, and American submarines had accounted for two of the Japanese carriers. Finally, in the last hours of daylight, U.S. carrier-borne aircraft also attacked the retreating enemy fleet, and in twenty minutes sank another carrier and damaged four more. The toll taken of Japanese pilots, especially, was catastrophic—Americans called it "the great Marianas turkey shoot".

The effects of this victory, coinciding as it did with the Japanese defeat in Burma, were considerable. On the day of the Saipan landings, Japan itself had been bombed by the new long-range American B-29s from China, and the loss of the Marianas (which was now inevitable) would give the Americans secure airfields from which they could strike regularly at Japanese cities. On July 18th 1944 General Tojo's government therefore resigned. However, his successors did not conclude that the war Tojo had begun was already lost. On the contrary, they reinforced the Ryukyu and Bonin Islands, and chose General Yamashita, conqueror of Malaya, to defend the Philippines against MacArthur, who had now completed the conquest of New Guinea. Nevertheless, Yamashita's chances were not good. His ten divisions would be outnumbered more than 4 to 1, and in any case were dispersed throughout the islands. Consequently, when it became clear that MacArthur's first target was Leyte, it fell to the Japanese navy and air force to attack the American armada and assist Yamashita to concentrate his troops.

It was a daunting prospect. The heavy casualties meant that the Japanese were now having to send up pilots who were little more than half-trained; losses had already reached suicidal proportions and fuel was short. Worse still, MacArthur's own fleet had been reinforced by the powerful 3rd Fleet under Admiral Halsey. But the risks had to be accepted. American submarines were already wreaking havoc among Japanese oil-tankers: if the Philippines were lost, Japan would be cut off from her oil supplies altogether and her fleet would be useless anyway. Toyoda decided to gamble everything. A decoy force of half-empty carriers was to lure Halsey away to the north, while seven Japanese battleships from Singapore, supported by cruisers and land-based aircraft, fell on MacArthur's weaker fleet and troop-transports in Leyte Gulf (October 1944). Up to a point the plan worked. Halsey took the bait and pursued the enemy carriers with his own, but not before sinking the giant battleship *Musashi* and shooting down over half the Japanese aircraft. MacArthur's fleet then successfully broke up a subsidiary surface attack, after which the remaining enemy—though within an ace of victory had they but known it—became anxious as to Halsey's whereabouts, and withdrew. Meanwhile, Halsey's foray against the Japanese carriers had resulted in all four being sunk, and thus ended the greatest naval battle of all time.

As a result, MacArthur's assault on the Philippines proceeded according to plan, despite the employment by a now desperate enemy of *Kamikaze* pilots—men ready to sacrifice their lives by crashing aircraft loaded with explosives on to American vessels. Leyte and Mindoro fell before the end of 1944. In January 1945, fresh troops of General Krueger's 6th Army landed on Luzon; Bataan and Corregidor were recaptured. In March U.S. Marines seized Iwo Jima in the Bonin Islands as a staging-post for American bombers. In April, General Buckner's 10th Army assaulted Okinawa, like Iwo Jima a veritable rabbit-warren of underground defences, desperately contested by the Japanese. The government which had replaced Tojo then resigned in its turn. Meanwhile the success of the Normandy landings had enabled the British to add a sizeable naval contribution in the Pacific to the continuing efforts of their troops in Burma, where Mandalay had fallen in March, and Rangoon was taken by amphibious assault in May. Nevertheless, with powerful armies still undefeated, the Japanese were not prepared to humiliate either their Emperor or themselves by accepting the Allied demand for unconditional surrender.

UNCONDITIONAL SURRENDER

The Yalta Conference

That demand was not the only political mistake made by the Allies. When the Big Three met again at Yalta in the Crimea, in February 1945, the ailing Roosevelt's belief in Stalin's goodwill, already apparent at Teheran, manifested itself once more. It was clear even then that Stalin intended to establish satellite Communist governments in some "liberated" countries. However, the western Allies had no wish to quarrel with Russia. Roosevelt insisted that Stalin was "not an imperialist", and the conference ended in agreeing to post-war zones of occupation which were to leave Germany divided and half of Europe firmly under Russian control. At the time there seemed no reason to doubt Stalin's good faith towards his own allies, and problems—like that of Berlin—which might arise later over these arrangements were not really foreseen. In return Stalin promised to join the war against Japan, hoping thereby to acquire parts of China!

The End in Europe

The fighting in Europe was now entering its final stages. In Italy, after months in which the struggle had degenerated into a dreary sideshow, Allied morale improved with the realisation that the tieing-down of enemy forces there had contributed significantly to the success of "Overlord". In April 1945 the Germans were routed in the open country bordering the Po river and surrendered on May 2nd. Mussolini, who after the Italian capitulation in 1943 had been dramatically rescued by German paratroops, was caught and lynched by his own countrymen.

In Germany there was mounting hysteria. A majority of Germans never actually belonged to the Nazi Party (any more than most Russians are Communist Party members), and while many Germans had supported Hitler in the days of his success, it became a different matter when his policies seemed certain to bring ruin

The Yalta Conference. Churchill, Roosevelt and Stalin.
(Imperial War Museum)

on their own country. Suspicion grew rapidly between the Party and the increasingly disillusioned armed forces. In July 1944 an unsuccessful bomb attempt had been made on Hitler's life by army officers, and after that Party organisations like the S.S. took over more and more of the responsibility for defence and security. Rommel, who was ordered to commit suicide, was one of their more distinguished victims.

Meanwhile, the German forces were being crushed between the twin steam-rollers of the eastern and western Allies. These last months of the war were the heyday of the bomber, as the Luftwaffe no longer had either the will or the fuel to resist effectively. The United States Air Force concentrated on bombing precise targets in daylight, the bombers being escorted by long-range fighters. Since the spring of 1944 they had concentrated on oil plants, at Ploesti in Rumania, and in Germany itself. By July that year every important German oil centre

May 1945. Hamburg on the day of its surrender.
(Imperial War Museum)

had been hit and the enemy's forces restricted to a tiny fraction of their real fuel
requirements. The R.A.F., however, raiding by night, aimed to devastate large
industrial areas, where air-raids were bound to cause heavy civilian casualties.
In the last quarter of 1944 Bomber Command dropped more bombs than in the
whole of 1943—60,000 tons of high explosive on the Ruhr alone—and in February
1945 the most controversial and devastating raid of the whole European war was
directed at Dresden, a beautiful and historic city already swarming with refugees.
German industry displayed remarkable resilience under this ordeal and production
was maintained.

   The air offensive meant that by early 1945 the German transport system was
in ruins, and organised resistance impossible for long. In the east, some 200
Russian divisions rolled forward from the Vistula in their American trucks. They
seized Silesia, Germany's last intact industrial area, and halted in February on the
line of the Oder/Neisse rivers. Hitler's attempts to counter-attack merely

facilitated a simultaneous western offensive which crossed the Rhine in March against generally scant opposition, encircled an entire Army Group in the Ruhr, and advanced to meet the Russians at Torgau on the Elbe on April 25th. Meanwhile, Stalin's failure to honour some of the promises made at Yalta had convinced the British that the western Allies should try to occupy Berlin before the Russians did, despite the agreement over zones of occupation. However, Eisenhower rejected this view, and his decision left the city to the Soviet forces. As they closed in towards the end of April, and even his favourite horoscope offered no hope, Hitler committed suicide. The squalid chapter was closed.

The Atomic Bomb

The war in Europe officially ended on May 8th 1945 ("V.E." Day), though German forces, anxious to avoid capture by the vengeful Russians, had actually been surrendering piecemeal for some time. To most families in Britain the "real" war now seemed over and the "forgotten army" in the Far East more remote than ever. Defeat for Japan, appallingly battered from the air in recent months, was certain. On a single night in March, 16 square miles of Tokyo had been burnt down by incendiary bombs, killing 83,000 people—many more than died in air-raids on Britain during the whole of the war. Yet the Emperor's forces fought fanatically on.

The stumbling-block was American insistence on unconditional surrender. But for this, the terrors of the atomic bomb need never have been unleashed at all, since a new Japanese government was already putting out peace feelers in July 1945, before the bomb was ready. However, both Russians and Americans ignored these because, suspicion having by now developed between the Allies in Europe, each wanted to end the war with a strong bargaining position in the Far East—the Russians by joining in before the defeat of Japan, and the Americans by dropping the atomic bomb to forestall them. This was the real reason for the use of the new weapon on Hiroshima and Nagasaki in August. Even so, its immediate effect has often been exaggerated. Japan could no better have withstood a repetition of "conventional" raids like that on Tokyo in March, and a more important factor in ending the fighting was a belated American agreement to respect the Emperor's sovereignty. Upon this, the Emperor himself insisted on surrender (August 14th) and the war was over.

All that remained was to pick up the pieces. The Russians, of course, had already picked up most of theirs. A third meeting of the Allied leaders, at Potsdam near Berlin in July 1945, came too late to change that, though the atomic bomb did foil a Russian demand to share in the occupation of Japan. Roosevelt had died in April, and Churchill was ousted at a General Election which took place while the conference was in progress; Stalin was the only one of the original "Big Three" to survive the war in possession, as it were. He used the advantage.

POSTSCRIPT

How can we summarise the reasons for the enemy's eventual collapse? First, their position was essentially weak from the beginning, provided the Allies did not succumb at once. Italy had to obtain virtually all war materials from abroad. The Germans lacked vital necessities like rubber, cotton, and nickel even after their conquests had partially eased the shortage of that still more essential commodity, oil. Japan was too heavily dependent on maintaining control of the sea. The enemy's chances therefore hung on rapid and complete victory, and it was that which made Britain's defiance in 1940-41, and the Americans' recovery after Pearl Harbour, so important. German war production, for example, was originally geared to short, sharp bursts of effort by limited sections of industry—one reason why the German navy was too weak either to defeat Britain in 1940, or to prevent the Allies drawing on resources from all over the world later on.

Secondly, taking the war as a whole, the Allies' resources were far greater and more efficiently mobilized—both of manpower and industrial production—than the enemy's. America's factories, for example, were able to supply all her own needs and a major part of her allies' as well, while in Britain a much higher proportion of the available labour force was directly engaged in the war effort than was the case in any other country.

Thirdly, the enemy made a number of serious strategic errors. In Germany's case, these were usually the product of Hitler's belief in his own infallibility, and a single example must suffice to make the point. In the later stages of the war, Germany's greatest weakness was the lack of any system of organised air defence. By 1943 the Germans could have had a jet aircraft (the Messerschmitt 262) and several kinds of ground-to-air missiles, the possession of which would certainly have destroyed the Allies' air superiority and made any invasion of Europe very difficult—yet Hitler decided instead to divert his resources to the production of the comparatively useless V-weapons. Japan's misplaced faith in battleships proved equally decisive.

Lastly, there is the moral angle. Atrocity has always been a part of war, but in modern times only Nazi Germany has embarked on a systematic policy of mass-slaughter. Nazism was a bankrupt philosophy founded on insecurity, envy and hatred: it had nothing constructive to offer when things went wrong. Japan, too, was misled by a false belief in her own superiority, based on her unbroken military success since becoming industrialised in the 19th century. Yet despite industrialisation, Japan remained at heart a medieval society, where the warrior was idolised and the ruling-class all-powerful. In their hatred of the foreigner, Japanese war-lords underestimated the resilience of more balanced systems than their own, and in the final analysis resilience is what matters most.

On the whole the Allies were quicker to profit from experience than their opponents, but the war saw many advances in military techniques on both sides. The German successes in the early part of the war were based on superior professional training in the manipulation of mobile armoured columns, and a recognition of the importance of air support for ground forces. The Allies, by contrast, were the first to appreciate the possibilities of supplying troops from the air—in Abyssinia and later in Burma. They also succeeded in the more ambitious field of combined operations, involving immense problems of co-operation between land, sea and air forces: the D-Day landings, for instance, were the triumphant culmination of months of study and trials by Earl Mountbatten's Combined Operations staff. At sea, the aircraft carrier and the submarine emerged from the war as the capital ships of our time, and the battleship, which had ruled the world's oceans since the days of the Spanish Armada, passed into history.

There were also the lessons of failure. Parachute troops, for example, lightly-armed as they were, had been shown to depend too heavily on luck for success in major operations. Hitler became convinced of this after the experience of Crete—an experience which probably saved Malta from a similar fate—but not altogether surprisingly, it took the Arnhem débâcle to persuade the Allies of the same thing. Much the same was true of bombing, the other great bogey of the pre-war years. The British Air Staff, under the influence of Air Marshal "Bomber" Harris of Bomber Command, believed emphatically in the value of "strategic bombing"—that is, the indiscriminate saturation of whole industrial areas as a means of terrorising the civilian population. Yet after the war it became clear that such raids had on the whole been less effective than those on specific military targets like the Ploesti oilfields, and had even been counter-productive in stiffening the enemy's will to resist.

However, perhaps the most obvious, and at the same time most important lesson to be learned from these tragic years, is that the price of peace is constant readiness for war. Hitler could afford to feel confident in the 1930s because he saw that his potential victims were divided, whereas the Germans were a united and—in their own way—patriotic people. Only in Britain, among European countries, was the spirit of old-fashioned patriotism still strong enough to overcome the jealousies of class divisions, and produce a united defence of the essential standards which that country represented and had done so much to create.

Postscript

Today, the world remains divided, more sharply than in 1939. For every wrong the war righted, it created others quite as great. The threat of Communism to the democracies now is probably no less menacing—if less immediate—than the threat of Fascism in the 1930s. In Europe, for example, countries which were once the victims of Nazi aggression are now under the heel of Russia. Attempts on their part to reassert the independence for which the war was supposedly fought, as in Hungary in 1956 or Czechoslovakia in 1968, have been suppressed with no less ruthlessness than Hitler would have shown.

For this state of affairs, President Roosevelt was partly responsible. In his apparent belief that the U.S.A., as a classless society, had more in common with Stalin's Russia than with the more aristocratic, imperial powers of western Europe, Roosevelt showed himself to be either remarkably gullible or remarkably cold-blooded: Stalin had been grooming his clients to take over in eastern Europe for several years. However, Roosevelt's successor, Harry Truman, was much less starry-eyed about Stalin's intentions, and the result was a noticeable cooling in relations between Russia and the West, particularly over the administration of Berlin. Before long the erstwhile allies were totally at loggerheads.

In short, the end of the war did not mean an end of the mass-misery it had caused. Refugees fled in their millions from the advance of Soviet Russia, and to this day many remain as "stateless persons", citizens of the world without a country. Many of Europe's surviving Jews, it is true, did find a new home in the freshly-created state of Israel, only to give birth to the Arab-Israeli conflict which is still going on. Germans suffered, too. After the war Germany was dismembered, split between East and West (Russia still refuses to sign a peace treaty with Germany as a whole), and obliged to hand back a good deal of territory to Poland and Czechoslovakia. In this process, some 10 million Germans were either uprooted or killed: the terms of Versailles seem charitable by comparison.

Moreover, the Allies' determination to crush German militarism together with Nazism, and their consequent refusal to come to terms with opponents of Hitler in the German Army, undoubtedly prolonged the war against Germany— thus contributing to the physical and economic exhaustion of Europe which in turn assisted the Communist takeover in eastern Europe. In the west, the result was dependence on American aid—a dependence which in the field of defence still continues, despite the efforts of General de Gaulle to establish Europe as a third force between the two super-powers. Consequently, it is worth reflecting that if the German armour had not been permitted to break through so easily in France in 1940, it must have been improbable that Hitler would have dared to attack Russia in 1941, and therefore unlikely that so much of Europe would have fallen under Communist domination after 1945. Most of Europe's post-war problems stem from this fact.

However, the profoundest changes wrought by the war occurred in Asia, where the most significant pointer for the future was not the dropping of the first atomic bomb, but the fall of Singapore to the Japanese. That one event destroyed the old-established belief in the white man's invincibility, and by demonstrating how vulnerable the European position in the East really was, encouraged the Asiatic peoples to seek a new status in the world when the war was over. In 1947 the British granted independence to India; two years later the old Dutch East Indian empire was reborn as the Republic of Indonesia; in 1954 the French were compelled to surrender their control over Indo-China. These changes, of course, transformed the relative importance of Europe as much as that of Asia.

Meanwhile, in China, Communist forces led by Mao Tse-Tung had by 1949 scored a complete victory over Chiang Kai-Shek's American-supported Nationalist government. Ironically, the Communist triumph was again made all the easier by American policy. Their insistence on removing Japanese occupying forces in 1945, before Chiang Kai-Shek had had a chance to re-establish control, left a vacuum of power eagerly filled by Mao Tse-Tung's men, and after four years of civil war Chiang was driven on to the island stronghold of Formosa, where he has remained ever since. By contrast, Japan—in whose name some appalling atrocities had been committed, in China and on the notorious Burma railway—escaped from the war comparatively lightly.

Indeed, the war's paradoxes were perhaps its most remarkable feature. The struggle which produced the atomic bomb also made possible the nuclear power station. The age of the extermination camp was likewise the age of penicillin. The loss of priceless art treasures must be weighed against the levelling of some unspeakable slums. The V-weapon was the forerunner of the space satellite. Even on a minor level, the pattern remains true. Aerial reconnaissance, which identified the V-weapon launching sites and was also the prelude to so much death and destruction from the air, is now an accepted part of the equipment with which the archaeologist seeks to resurrect what the past has destroyed.

Thus the horrors of war may give rise to a time of hope. The fear of nuclear conflict has compelled the great powers, at least, to exercise restraint in their dealings with one another. In another respect, too, there is some reason for optimism: the enforced co-operation between allies brought about by the war has already been carried over into voluntary collaboration between nations at peace. The international response which now follows any great natural disaster, for example, would have been unthinkable in the 1930s, and the work of such agencies as W.H.O., U.N.E.S.C.O. and U.N.I.C.E.F. has given a new dimension to the meaning of "civilisation". All the same, it is wise to remember that human nature does not seem to change very much. The optimist is still a man who believes all is for the best in the best of all possible worlds—and the pessimist still fears he may be right.